SHAKESPEARE

A Boy's Tale

Scott Pixello

Publisher Information

Published by Scott Pixello

Copyright © 2016
Scott Pixello

Cover Design: www.candescentpress.co.uk

The Globe illustration (adapted) by C. Walter Hodges courtesy of the Folger Shakespeare Library. Shared under CC BY-SA 4.0

Author's Note

There is very little consensus on the appearance, the signature, even the very existence of William Shakespeare. Many aspects of Shakespeare's life often taken as 'fact' are actually based on little or no evidence at all. This book is a work of fiction, which weaves together what is possible with our best source of evidence- the plays themselves. It is not written in Shakespearean English, which would be largely incomprehensible to a twenty-first century reader. If you do like Shakespearean English, I recommend the plays. Except perhaps, *Timon of Athens*.

It should also be noted that dates have been adjusted to the Gregorian calendar as we are now familiar with it, post 1752.

'O this learning, what a thing it is!'
(*The Taming of the Shrew*, Act I (ii), l. 130)

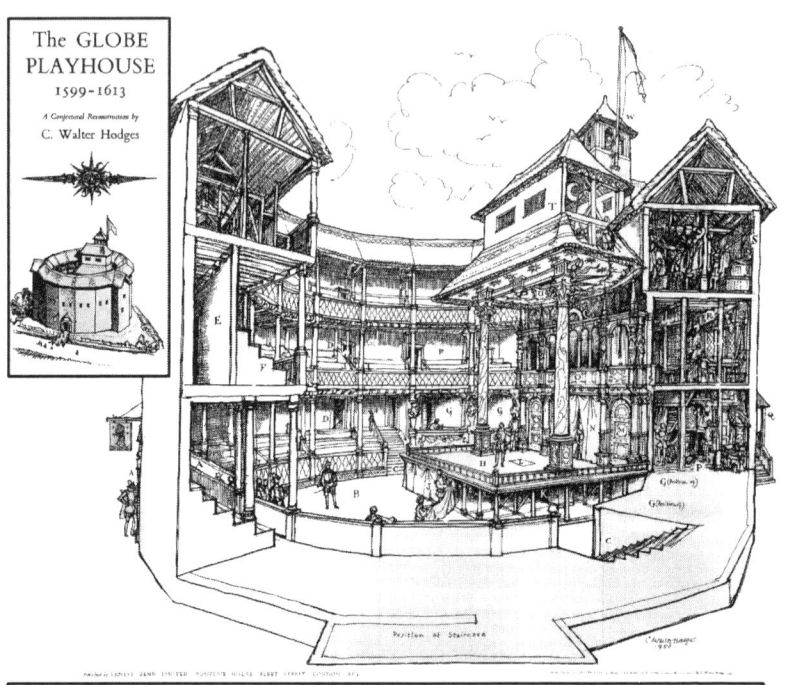

The GLOBE
PLAYHOUSE
1599–1613

A Conjectural Reconstruction by
C. Walter Hodges

KEY

Chapter One

Trapped

'They have tied me to the stake, I cannot fly
But bear-like I must fight the course.'
(*Macbeth*, V, (vi), l.1-2)

"Oi, beggar-boy, what jew fink you're dewin?" A shadow fell across Tom's pale face and he looked up and froze. The owner of the voice had a neck that was thicker than his bald head and a vivid scar down one cheek that he probably hadn't got from selling fruit. He was very ugly, very strong and spotting the boy's hand as it reached out to grab a tempting rosy apple, he looked like he would peel him too if got the chance. Tom gave a sheepish smile and backed away slowly, the stallholder scowling at him.

It was Friday and the markets on London's South Bank were teeming with people and filled with the noise of squawking chickens and vendors calling out their wares. The crowds were thick with folk on their way to The Globe, a playhouse which could be seen in the distance, a flag flying, showing that there would be a performance today. Fresh produce, including fish taken straight from the Thames, surrounded the beggar-boy on every side. Mouth-watering smells of spit-roasted hog and freshly-baked cinnamon cakes filled the air. Instinctively Tom put his hand to his stomach. He hadn't eaten for two days.

He had decided to hang around the bear-baiting arena. At the height of a particularly dramatic fight and with the skill of someone who had spent most of their life on the streets, he managed to slip in unnoticed by the burly 'gatherer' at the main door. The attention of the men, most of whom were drunk, was firmly on a poor animal, chained to a large post in a pit and the dogs that were set upon it, sometimes one at a time, sometimes together. The bear, a magnificent creature, ten feet high when it stood on its huge back legs, had suffered some nasty wounds and it looked unlikely to survive the day. Gawping at such a beautiful creature being ripped to pieces for money was not something Tom could ever imagine doing for fun. But it did mean he could move around without being noticed. After only a few minutes, he needed some fresh air and went out again.

The 'nipping' or 'dipping' gangs worked the markets by the river. Their method was fairly straightforward, targeting bags or purses, which could be taken without detection as few garments had pockets. This was often done by means of an extremely-sharp short knife-hence they were also referred to as 'cutpurses.' Tom had a knife, of course, everyone did but he didn't like having to carry it and had never used it in a fight. At least, not yet. Violent fights and stabbings, even between the thieves themselves, were a frequent occurrence. The really skilful thieves, 'the foists' as they were known, could take purses without the rich merchants or their wives noticing a thing.

Tom wanted to be in the gang. Not because he enjoyed the company of the leader, a nasty piece of work called Jack, or the others or that he enjoyed the act of stealing. He just wanted to feel that he belonged somewhere. And he didn't want to starve.

He edged closer to a young woman buying fruit and peered over her shoulder. She was picking up individual apples, inspecting them, sighing and then putting them back as if every spending decision was hard. He stretched a little more and caught a glimpse of something else- a baby, no more than a few days old, nestling within the folds of his mother's dress, with only his tiny face visible. At that precise moment, the blue eyes of the tiny face locked onto his and held him.

He desperately looked back at where Jack was slouching by an ale stall. He ran several gangs of pickpockets and creamed off most of the takings for himself. Nearby growled a scrawny little dog called Nipper, who he kicked from time to time, just about kept alive on scraps and always talked of selling to the baiting-pits to fight.

"Go on," he hissed, seeing Tom's hesitation. "Get on with it, Swanny." Jack was always at him. Any little way to annoy him- talking about his family, his clothes, even his name. 'Look at him, swanning around as if he's something special,' or 'Tom Swann, Tom Swann- see that long neck with an ugly face on.' It wasn't exactly poetry but the other thieves in the gang often joined in, more out of fear of Jack than actively hating him but that didn't make it any better. They said that a swan's wings could break a man's legs. Unfortunately, he didn't feel that strong.

"I...can't," Tom stuttered, still held by the baby's huge blue eyes.

"Well," scoffed Jack. "If you won't, I will. Here, out the way." He marched forward, shoved Tom roughly aside and reached for the woman's small purse with a knife. It was only inches from the baby's face.

"NO!" cried Tom and pushed back, knocking into the surprised woman and luckily not leading to either mother or child being stabbed.

"Why, you little-" began Jack and in anger lashed out with the knife. Tom sprang back but he was caught on the left forearm and a red line appeared through his tunic.

The woman whirled round and seeing the blood, started to scream the word that froze Tom to his marrow: "THIEF!"

The wound wasn't deep enough to hurt much but at that single word, Tom reacted as if he'd been burned and he dived into where the crowd was thickest, seeking safety in numbers.

"THIEF!" That single word was enough to make all the stallholders' ears prick up. Only "FIRE!" made them move faster. Anyone who could, man woman or child, always joined the chase. If they acted together, they mostly caught the thief, usually a beggar and made sure he was suitably punished- often at the end of a rope. The hue and cry that followed was like a wildfire, slow at first but fanned by other cries, it soon grew into an unstoppable force that seemed to move faster than his legs could carry him. The stall-keepers kept a careful watch for thieves, especially around midday when the crowds were larger. He had only one way out-run.

He pushed through people as if trying to make forward progress through a dense wood. A mob had already formed and the shouting behind him exploded. "Thief! There! Over there!"

His heart was racing but it was like swimming upstream and his arms were soon starting to drop and he began to gasp for breath. He pulled the hood on his coat even further up, which was all very well but then he couldn't really see where he was going. He crashed into people, who turned, their eyes a mixture of surprise and anger. It was the same in every direction and the ridiculous disguise that Jack, his so-called friend, had persuaded him to use only made matters worse. Oh, why had he listened to him? Jack always made things sound so easy but the truth was Tom was always the one expected to try out the latest ideas. And the first one to get caught.

The bald man's voice rang out. "I'm gonna cairnt to free and if you don't give yourself up, boy, I'm sending me dog in after ya. One!" He didn't really have a dog, did he? "Two." Come on, come on, think of something fast. "Right then, I'm coming in after you. Free."

The market stretched down the high street, south from the bridge and included a small hall where produce could be weighed. Pitches were officially-allocated and often there were bitter disputes between stallholders, leading to arguments and fights. It was not only a Friday market day but Mayday, swelling the crowds still further with revellers come to see the dancing round the maypole, the costumed Green Man and all the eating and drinking associated with this time of plenty. Unfortunately, for Tom, it was not a time to celebrate. Begging had become more difficult recently with harsh laws introduced, designed to end the practice. Or end the lives of beggars, thought Tom grimly. He was a problem the nobility would like to be rid of.

There were dice and card-games in progress on each street-corner with men crowded round, some genuine potential customers but some, Tom knew, positioned as part of the gang to lure in their prey. There was also at least one look-out in case a Constable was on patrol. They might be figures of fun but at his age, 13, he could be forced to become an apprentice or perform other unpleasant work. Those running the games, the so-called 'coneycatchers' talked endlessly while their hands moved at lightning speed over the dice or cards or cups or whatever the mechanism was to cheat their victims ('the coneys'). There were jugglers, musicians and even a fortune teller's tent. He heard running footsteps. They might not be his pursuers but he couldn't take that chance and in desperation, he ducked swiftly inside.

It was almost pitch dark and it took a second for his eyes to adjust to the gloom.

"Well, come in, if you're coming," said a voice from the far end, which seemed strangely bigger inside than he had expected. He took a few tentative steps forwards.

Into view came a table and seated at the table was an incredibly old woman. Well, she looked incredibly old. Most people over 20 looked old to Tom, but so few people lived beyond 50, he rarely saw truly old people.

His eyes wandered over her a bit like he had been observing the bear outside, as if she was an entirely different species. The woman had frizzy, grey hair beneath a headscarf, claw-like hands and- he froze as her eyes flicked up to him. She had incredible, deep-green eyes, the like of which he'd never seen and for a moment, he felt his chest contract as if she saw into his very soul.

She didn't speak further but gestured to him to sit in a chair opposite. Now he saw a pack of cards on the table, which she picked up and began to lay out. This was not a pack like the coney-catchers used to cheat people. There were pictures of skeletal figures and situations he couldn't recognise, partly because it was still dim at this end of the tent, despite the presence of a flickering candle on the table, which cast a ghostly dancing shadow of the old crone's head on the wall behind.

She still didn't speak, although now he was aware of her raspy breathing. There was just the slap of cards being turned over and given a slight snap as she laid them with careful precision in a diamond formation.

She stopped and looked up. "Give me your hand," she snapped, in a tone that was more command than invitation. Tom instinctively did what he was told without really knowing why. He stretched out his arm and was surprised by the strength of the woman's grip as she took his hand in her own. It was strange. She hadn't demanded money or even asked his name. Maybe she was going to tell him, he thought with a bit of a smirk.

She pulled his arm a little towards her, so she could see his palm in the light. What she saw there seemed to puzzle her as she traced a few lines, which tickled a little. She frowned and rubbed as if wanting to make sure that what she was looking at wasn't just dirt.

That was a fair point. He hadn't exactly expected to find himself in this situation and the last thing he'd been touching were some less-than-pristine apples. She eventually released his hand.

"Is there a…problem?" His own voice sounded stupid to him, high-pitched and slightly effeminate.

She turned certain cards over, still without speaking and drew others towards her.

"You are an unusual boy," she said eventually. "According to your palm, you are close to your mother and you work hard. And yet-"

"-Yes?"

She sighed. "According to the cards, you are a…thief." She spoke that last word with some venom.

"Well, I, er," he began, since it was his intention to become a good one. Not because of greed but to survive and more importantly, to find a way to provide for his sick mother. She lay in bed, with a hideous racking coughing and rarely got up any more. It was up to him to put bread on the table. Stealing wasn't his choice and he knew it was wrong but so was starving to death. Tom had been brought up to believe in and fear God but privately, he could not understand a God who would let people like him, good people for the most part, starve to death while others rode around in carriages, living lives of sin and corruption.

"And," continued the woman, who was still staring at him as if she couldn't quite square what she was looking at. "Sometimes the cards and palms do not tally. But…not like this." She selected another card. It showed a picture of a woman, about his height with soft delicate features. "Do you have a wife?" He almost laughed out loud. He was only thirteen. But he saw she was serious and so shook his head. "There will be women in your future."

There were three cards in the centre of her formation. It seemed they were the most important. One-by-one she turned them round to face him. "The Magician, the Hanged Man and the Fool." She stared directly at him. "Which one are you?"

He looked at the cards in shock. His future was looking fairly bleak. He'd certainly been a fool with Jack and trying to get into the dipping gangs. If he was caught, he might well find himself at the end of a rope but Magician? There was precious little magic in his life right now.

He also now felt like the Fool for coming in here and especially since he remembered something else- he had no money with which to pay for this strange reading. Not a bean. Which would only confirm her view of him as a thief no doubt.

"But, you must decide which of these you are…Tom." His mouth dropped open. "It is of no consequence how or why I know these things. The stars have set out a destiny for you but you must work your will to make things happen as they are foretold."

Mumbling an apology for having no money, he almost ran out of the tent, oblivious to the danger potential outside. His legs were driven by fear of the witch-like crone and her more-than-mortal knowledge of his fate.

He careered straight into the crowd which had grown even bigger in the last few minutes and allowed himself to be carried along like a leaf on a stream, until he could tack across to a line of carts, parked next to the river. There was no sign of the hue and cry but he needed some time to calm himself.

He dodged in between the nearest cart and having no other choice, crawled beneath it, squeezed his eyes shut and prayed that he had somehow magically become invisible. For a few terrible seconds, time seemed to stand still and he just tried to breathe but his heartbeat grew so loud he was sure everyone else could hear it.

On the other side of the cart, the side next to the river, a pair of legs walked slowly past and then stopped inches from his face. This was it. He was done for.

Suddenly, a face appeared looking sideways beneath the cart and a heavy hand dropped on his shoulder, a dagger of ice gripped his heart and as he turned, he was met by the words, "Allo my little Tommy, got me apples, ave you?"

The apparently-friendly speaker half-dragged the boy out from his hiding-place. The cart was parked up against a low wall that ran along by the river but there was a narrow gap, just wide enough for one person to pass, and it was in that space where the two figures now stood. However, far from being grateful, the boy stood up and angrily pushed his rescuer away.

It was only Jack who looked older than his 15 years and although he was wasn't as tall as Tom, he had the beginnings of a beard and there was the bulge of some muscles beneath his rough tunic. Like all bullies, he had an apparent unchallengeable belief in his own strength-something Tom definitely lacked.

"Idiot," muttered Tom. He risked a quick look round but as far as could be seen the chasing pack had gone or given up. For now.

"Hey, that's not very nice. Besides," Jack gave a sadistic laugh. "You was scared."

"I was not. It was…just a stupid disguise. I could have been caught a million times."

"But it worked, didn't it? Told you it would. A tall lad like you, a hessian robe, put on a funny voice and Bob's your uncle. Or your aunt, in this case."

"It was sheer luck."

"Come on, you big girl," Jack clicked his big meaty fingers. "Hand em over." Tom slowly fished the apples out of his shirt. A couple more had come out during the chase and those that were left looked battered and bruised but no less than his ribs which had taken a beating in forcing his way through the crowd.

"You can do it yourself next time." He had recovered his breath a little by now and what was left was anger. He'd taken the risk and here was Jack as usual taking all the credit. Just because he was two years older didn't mean he was right about everything.

"Oh no. I fink you've shown a real talent for this sort of fing."

"What about my share?"

"Share? Oh, right. Course." He tossed over the last apple of the lot- smaller than the rest and a little bruised.

"What's this?"

"I would ave thought wiv all your learning, you'd know that." Jack despised his attempts to read. As far as he was concerned, books were for priests or noblemen, not the likes of them.

"I know what it is. I mean, why have I only got one?"

Jack slowly came closer and Tom's confident bluster ebbed away with each step. Jack pushed his face right into his. "Because, you see…I'm me. And you, well…you're just you." Tom could see the muscles standing out on Jack's arms, the snarl of his lips and most frightening of all, the leering, empty hatred in his pale-blue eyes. "What else can you do?"

"I…I….I."

Jack just mimicked his voice, which always turned high-pitched when Tom got angry, making him even more angry and more like a squeaky mouse. "Cat got ya tongue ?" he laughed. "Fought so. What you can do, my friend, is keep quiet and run back to your muvva like you always do." At the mention of his mother, Tom felt his face flush bright red and his fingers instinctively clenched into a fist. "Look at ya. What are ya, 11? 12?"

"13," he mumbled.

"13? By your age, I was a prentice to a smivy. What trade have ya got then, eh?" He seized one of Tom's arms and gave it a squeeze as if he was a prize cow. "Not much there. You'll need to fill aht a bit if ya want to earn a living." He flexed an arm to show what was missing. "That's what you need, not wasting ya time trying to get above yourself wiv books an' 'at. Where's that ever gonna get ya?" He shook his head. "Just coz you talk all proper. You fink you're be'er than me."

"No," replied Tom, but without much conviction.

"Well, you're not. You're just a beggar like the rest of us. Look at cha. What ope is there for you? Farva, a no-good coward and a muvva, well, the best fing is for you to run off to your crippled muvva, beanpole Tommy. She's all you've-"

-He was about to say "got" but his round face was suddenly met Tommy's balled-up fist and despite the age difference, anger added about 10 years to the punch.

"Aghh" Jack staggered back, in shock as much as pain, almost falling off the bridge. "Why, you little-" and he made a grab for Tom, who luckily, was just too quick and skipped out of range.

He ran and ran until his lungs felt ready to burst and his vision swam. He slipped along the muddy road past wagons of traders on their way to and from the market but he could still hear his pursuer screaming in the distance. But Jack was older and stronger. In the end, he'd be sure to catch him.

Tom dodged behind a wagon to try and catch his breath. Peering out carefully, he could see Jack racing towards him, shoving people out the way, like a hunting dog that had scented its prey. He was trapped.

He was afraid- not just of being caught but what he had just done. What did he think he was doing hitting Jack Smethick? Now he couldn't work his way into the dipping gangs who worked the markets like he'd hoped. That was all that lay between his family and starvation. And for what?

Just because that loud-mouth idiot had called his father a coward. Well, as far as he knew, that was true. He could only dimly remember what he even looked like. Tom spent hours at night sometimes trying to picture his face but he was more a vague blurry shape, stooping down to him. His father was always picking him up. His arms were strong- he hadn't forgotten that or the smell of his coat, when he carried him on his shoulders. But everything else was just a haze and then he went off to fight in France and Tom never saw him again. The other men in his group or 'band' as they were known, many of whom had been 'pressed' to join up against their will, either died in battle or returned wounded but stories swirled around about his father's disappearance, along with the horses he was supposed to have been guarding. And as for his mother, well, she was a cripple, wasn't she? Stuck in a tiny, little one-room house all day, unable to move without pain, completely reliant on her only son to bring home something to eat and even more important, a sense of hope. What were they going to do now?

The back of the nearest cart was open and more out of exhaustion than cunning, he climbed in without thinking and pulling an empty sack over him, crouched down. Through a tiny gap in the sack he slowly peeked out but could see little.

Suddenly Jack's face lurched into view. He too was pausing to catch his breath, taking great gulps of air and cursing loudly. Then he glanced up and for a split second seemed to be looking right at Tom who froze for what seemed like an age, hardly daring to breathe. Jack just kept staring as his breathing eased and after a moment he spat and then ran on, still chuntering to himself about what he'd do to Tom when he caught him.

The cart was filled with a slightly hypnotic, yeasty smell and several sacks of what felt like flour or grain. Exhausted from the chase and mainly flooded with a sense of relief at escaping both the stallholder, the witch-like fortune teller and then Jack, he pulled another empty sack over himself and was suddenly hit by a wave of tiredness. He felt like a sailor lost at sea, who'd just seen a shark swimming inches below him and after a few deep breaths, sleep swallowed him up.

He woke some time later, aware of two things: the sounds of several voices and that the cart, which had been moving, had come to a stop. Blinking hard, he raised the flap a little. What met his gaze was a round, open space and what looked like wooden seats beyond. Was he still asleep? Was this some dream of a Roman amphitheatre that the boys told stories about? Then he heard voices more clearly and knew at once that he was not dreaming nor in Rome.

"All I'm saying is that if you seriously want you-know-who to look at you, you're going to have to develop some talent. Look, Jake, will you take some of the weight- I'm carrying it all here."

He spied two boys, both of whom seemed a little younger than himself. One was dark-haired and quite small, while the other was blond, a little tubby and seemed to be using only one hand to carry the bench they were lifting between them. He seemed more interested in what he held in the other.

"Cuthbert says," the larger boy boasted, "if I try hard I could be a leading player in a few years."

His friend scoffed. "And you don't think he was joking?" There was a pause as the first speaker didn't seem to have considered the possibility. "Look, I don't think you're going to be a leading anything if you don't know how to put in a day's work."

"Not my fault Henry," the first one mumbled, apparently with something in his mouth. "I'm hungry. It's only a drumstick."

"Jake, you're always hungry," muttered his mate. "Look, will you take the weight otherwise I'll drop this and then Burbage will roast you over a fire like the hog you are."

"Alright, alright. Can we put this down for a moment? It weighs more than your mother."

There was a crunching sound as the bench was half-put and half-dropped on what sounded like sand. "Besides," said the blond boy, clearing his throat, "I can drink more ale than most boys my age."

"And that's a talent, is it?" Jake started making a strange noise. "Is that your impression of Burbage? Sounds more like you dying." His partner started coughing and spluttering. "Yes, that's it. I'm sure the ladies will be very impressed." Jake started waving his arms around.

Henry put his hands on his hips, unimpressed. "Is this some kind of jest?"

Jake dropped his chicken to the ground and continued to make strangled, choking sounds, trying to make Henry understand that he couldn't breathe. By this time, his face had gone blue and he fell to his knees.

Without thinking, Tom scrambled out of the back of the cart, pushed past the bemused Henry and quickly assessed the situation. There were other men there, who he hadn't been able to see from the back of the cart but they too were just standing, frozen in shock.

Tom swiftly located a spot right in the middle of the choking boy's back and gave it a sudden, hard slap with the palm of his hand. This knocked the blond boy forward and something flew from his mouth, landing with a rather dramatic thud on the sand of the yard some feet away. While Jake started gasping violently for breath, like a shipwrecked sailor, the others crowded round to inspect the object. It was a small, innocent-looking chicken-bone.

The group turned back to Tom. A slight figure who seemed in charge stepped towards him. "What did you just do?"

Tom shrugged. "It was something my mother taught me."

"She sounds like a wise woman."

"She is."

Those who had come to see what the fuss was, crowded round Tom and he received several slaps on the back (although not quite as hard as the one he had given) for what they now realised, was a swift action that had saved their friend's life.

"What's your name, boy?" asked the man in charge who Tom guessed was the 'Cuthbert' he had heard about.

"Tom…Thomas."

"Thomas what?"

In the excitement of saving the boy's life, they seem to have forgotten that he was hiding in the cart and if he didn't answer swiftly, their attention might stray back to that. On the other hand, he didn't want to use his real name. He wasn't embarrassed about 'Swann' despite Jack's teasing. He'd only stolen a few apples but they hung thieves for less. At that moment, strangely, it wasn't fear of that that made him hesitate but the fear of bringing shame on his mother. He looked around at the empty seats.

"Well?" Cuthbert looked round at the others. "You don't know your own name?" Tom now saw that although the man's stature was slight, he had a short beard, a no-nonsense manner and there was steel in his voice. It was a voice that was used to being obeyed.

"Er…I," he hesitated. "…Shakespeare," he blurted out.

"What?"

"That's right, my name is…Thomas Shakespeare."

There was a second or two of absolute silence as if time stood still and then the whole group, including Jake and Henry, exploded into laughter, a sound that echoed round the empty seats.

Tom's face burned red and his hands balls themselves into fists. "I don't see that is any laughing matter." He was sounding like a humourless teacher and the laughter rang out even louder at his show of petulance.

Eventually, the merriment subsided and Cuthbert beckoned him over. "Well Thomas, there's someone here I think you should meet." A heavy hand fell on Tom's shoulder, making him jump. He turned to be faced by a tall stranger with very formal expression. "Sir," Cuthbert said, addressing the dark figure who'd been standing behind them all this time, calmly observing the scene. "I'd like you to meet Thomas Shakespeare." He turned back to the boy. "Tom, may I present…your father."

Chapter Two

A New World at The Globe

'Let us sit upon the ground and tell sad stories.'
(*Richard II*, III, (ii), l. 155)

Tom looked up. The face that met his seemed at first like many of the time. There was a beard, formally-cut and short, dark hair that seemed tousled rather than brushed. A single ear-ring gleamed for a second but this wasn't some pirate from the stories his mother used to tell him at bedtime. The figure to whom he had just been introduced was dressed all in black, which was unusual. Dyes were expensive and coloured material, including black, was usually only worn by noblemen.

What held Tom's gaze were the deep, dark eyes that seemed to bore into him. After a moment, the eyes seemed to find enough to welcome and the mouth came on board with a generous and open smile. Tom opened and closed his mouth like a fish but nothing came out.

"Cuthbert does like his little jokes. I'm Will. I try and keep this unruly bunch in some sort of order." Those piercing eyes looked at him intently. "Are you alright? You look like you've seen a ghost." Tom managed a nod. "Where did you learn that?" He nodded towards Jake who was being carried out.

"Oh, I…er…I read…something."

"You can read?" He looked at Tom in disbelief like he'd made a pig disappear.

He nodded. "My mother used to help me read a page of the Bible every week in church. Before she got ill anyway."

"Are you looking for a job?" Tom nodded eagerly. Will held his gaze a few seconds longer.

"The life we lead might seem devil-may-care but it is hard. We make ready five different plays a week. You have to learn lines, rehearse, prepare the stage and clean it up afterwards. You may be many things here- an actor, a reader, a writer, a maker of costumes and props, a dancer, a singer, a comic or indeed all of these. Most of us play several parts in a single play. The list is endless. The one thing you cannot be here is lazy. There are punishments for missing rehearsals, being late, even wearing costumes outside the building. Still interested?" Tom blew out his cheeks but still nodded. "Maybe we can find something for you to do here. I'm not promising anything but the most important thing is to make yourself useful. Do you like the theatre?"

Tom looked round. "It's...nice."

"I don't mean just this building, which, for your information, is much more than 'nice.' I mean," he made a sweeping gesture with his hands towards the stage. "The theatre."

Tom knew little of the world of players. Of course, he'd seen the morality plays performed by local groups of workers or guilds on temporary stages that would appear for a few days as a diversion for the people and with the approval of the Church as these 'mystery plays' as they were known, were usually stories from the Bible. There were dramatic royal processions when there was some significant occasion as there had been a couple of years before when James had become King on the death of Elizabeth. But the idea of a fixed place where people paid to see players- that was as alien to him as a journey to the moon.

"I...don't know. I've never been here before. At least I don't think so."

"Never been? Dear me. Well, bring your stuff round the back. You do have belongings?" Tom looked down at his sorry-looking tunic. "Never mind. The man who has nothing must be able to dream. Can you dream, Thomas?" He put a hand on his shoulder but he didn't flinch. "Well, anyway, if you can make yourself as useful as you have so far, then you are very welcome here. I should introduce the

15

company. We do not have one man in charge, telling everyone what to do."

"We don't?" said Cuthbert in mock surprise. "I thought that was your job."

The rest of the cast laughed. Clearly, Will liked to 'help' his fellow players with their performances. "Of course, you must forgive me," continued Will. "You are still surrounded by a group of strangers. Well, this is The King's Men. Look at the faces. Yes, I know, some are more pleasant than others but taken in the round they are not too pox-ridden."

The company were sitting at two of the benches that had been in the process of being carried in. "These are just for our next production but they should take your weight."

He started at the head of one of the extemporised tables and worked his way round. "That's Burbage and Cuthbert. They're brothers," he added. "Then there's Armin, Heminges, Condell, Sly, Cowley, Gough, Ned and-"

"-Now, now, Will, can't you see, the boy is overwhelmed. Come and sit down here. Names will come soon enough." The man who had spoken and had who waved Tom to join them at the table was the Heminges of the list which had just flown past Tom. He tried to catch one or two others but it was like stumbling upon a flock of birds and most had flown free.

Heminges waved him to come and sit at a vacant spot, which Tom willingly did. "Don't mind Will. He likes to think that everyone's head works like his." The man made a circular motion with his finger next to his forehead and grinned. Tom smiled too. "I'm John Heminges but everyone just calls me 'Heminges.'" He was like many of the group, a little older than Tom expected, somewhere around 50, fairly portly of build and a face covered with wrinkles. They mostly looked like laugh-lines as the man smiled a good deal and his energy and friendliness were that of a younger man than his grey, wispy hair suggested.

"A couple of names will suffice for today. Mine, of course as the most important in the company." Here there were jeers and whistles. "There are some jealous folk among us but they know that to be true.

And Burbage, of course." He waved at the slightly younger man at the head of the table. "Burbage always remains as 'Burbage' on account of his great theatrical family, his great ability to render tragic heroes but most of all the great opinion he has of himself." Burbage started to rise with an expression that could curdle milk. "Now, now, twas but a jest. See, boy how passionate the man is."

Burbage resumed his seat, if not his good temper, one hand stroking his sharp-pointed beard, looking every inch the evil tyrant from a play.

"Don't be fooled by his red-hair," whispered Heminges. "His temper is uncommonly mild but we have been rehearsing very hard these last few days and he has more lines to learn than there are stars in the sky. Next to him there sits William Sly, who often plays our gallants." The man in question raised a slightly sad-looking eye in Tom's direction. He was a good decade younger than Burbage with a pale complexion, brown curly hair and the faintest of moustaches.

"And of course," continued Heminges. "Will, you know. Well, as far as any of us do. That will do for introductions. Have you hunger?"

"Well-" began Tom but before he could answer, a giant bowl of soup was put down in front of him with bread and cheese on a side plate. "I have no money," Tom protested. "I can't-"

"-That's all good," said Will, holding up a hand." Do not fret, Master Swann. You have saved a life today. Although between us, I'm not sure if you'll receive any thanks from the party concerned. That is your payment. Eat, drink, restore yourself. Make yourself at home."

After being pleasantly full, the company relaxed with pipes and some strong wine. Tom sipped a little but it made his head swim.

"Now, who will tell us a story?" challenged Heminges. As Tom was to discover, almost everyone was an aspiring actor and always had a story to tell. "What about the murder of Kit Marlowe?"

A shadow passed over Will's face. "Too sad."

"Why, what happened to him?" blurted out Tom, before realising how rude that might sound.

"He was a playwright," explained Will. "A very good one. He was stabbed in a fight in Deptford. In 93." There was a pause. "He could

17

have achieved so much, poor fellow. No, I want to hear of something that dispatches my dark thoughts, not brings them on." He turned to his right. "Perhaps Richard, you could start? One for our newest recruit here."

Burbage nodded and settled himself, waiting for all eyes to fall on him.

"My father, James Burbage, was a great man. Imagine if you will someone who had something of my countenance, a little of my personality but none of my modesty." The company laughed. They knew the younger Burbage had plenty of vanity of his own. But with good reason too- it was his name on the lips of the growing crowds that flocked to playhouses. He was the player they came to see. It was his tragic heroes who reduced them to tears. He was the best known player of the company and it was his performances, especially of tragic heroes that drew the biggest crowds. His Hamlet, his Henry V, his Othello- that was what people talked about as they made their home at the end of a performance. Many of them also knew the tenacity of Burbage's father in business. Without his skills, the very fabric of their lives would not exist. It was a debt none of them forgot.

"Before my father died, far too soon, in 97, he was probably the first to see what playhouses could be. As a place of dreams and as a place where it was possible, given hard work, skill and not a little luck, that money could be made. It was he who established the first permanent theatre called appropriately enough, The Theatre, a word which others seem content to follow, to the north in Shoreditch, well-placed just beyond the city walls and next to a busy thoroughfare to take advantage of passing trade.

"He it was who was also the first to demand payment at the door. They used to pass a box round at the end of a performance but as you can imagine, that did not yield a fraction of the sums we can command here. For many years we had a successful company there, the Lord Chamberlain's Men, and it was this company that Will joined when he came down from Stratford.

"Now, my father leased the site from one Giles Allen. But when the time came to renew the lease, Allen refused, having decided apparently he no longer wanted a 'disreputable' playhouse on his land." This provoked some wry chuckles. The company knew only too well the low esteem in which players were held by those in power. "My father argued, threatened, even pleaded," continued Burbage, "but all to no avail.

"So, he planned to move to Blackfriars and establish a playhouse there. It was inside the city walls, the land was affordable and there was a ready audience near at hand. However, this plan was also blocked. Several well-to-do inhabitants used influence with the Privy Council to impede its progress. So what could he do? His existing business had no future and now all his hopes for an alternative, on which he'd spent months of time and not a little energy, lay like a broken vase shattered into a thousand pieces." Will smiled slightly at such an image too obvious for his own writing.

Tom shook his head. He had been drawn in by the tale despite himself.

"Well, arguments continued, even after his death. I and my brother Cuthbert," he nodded to his mirror image sitting across from him, "sought legal settlement. This continued for three years until Allen eventually gave up.

"In that time, we laid new plans. We leased some land here on the South Bank, not far from The Rose and employed the services of a fine carpenter by the name of Peter Street." At this point, Burbage lowered his voice and leaned forward as if to impart a vital secret. All the listeners instinctively craned their heads in too. "Now, we had a special and secret mission for Mr Street, one for which he was uniquely qualified.

"Imagine the situation. We now have the land and the company, a successful one but we have no building and no money to construct one. So what do we do? We couldn't get the necessary oak timbers, not without considerable expense and inconvenience. So we did the next best thing."

"What was that?" Tom asked, blurting out the question before he realised how rude it was.

Burbage smiled at how his lure had worked. "We stole them."

"Stole?"

"Yes."

"From where?"

"From our own theatre, of course. We took our old playhouse back. We had to choose our moment carefully and waited until Allen was out of town. Then we seized our chance.

It was the night of 28th December." He put out his hand in front of him and Tom instinctively followed his gaze as if the city was in the air before them. "The city was still consumed with celebrations for Christmas and the New Year and there were few people on the street, except for those hurrying home to be with their families.

"This was our plan: myself, Cuthbert and Street would demolish The Theatre. That's right, take it completely to pieces and then, over several days and under cover of darkness, transport these pieces, some on carts and some on boats across the frozen river, for it was perishing cold, over to the new site here where we are sitting right now. The Globe."

"How…how was it that you were not detected?" Tom tried and failed to keep the note of disbelief out of his voice.

"Well, yes, unfortunately Allen got wind of what we were doing and sent some of his workmen to stop us. There was…a difference of opinion, shall we say," he said with a roguish smile. Burbage and the others were not averse to drinking freely at local taverns and if disputes arose, settling them with their fists if necessary. It wasn't a regular occurrence but a spectacular success might be followed by a celebration. The following day, Burbage would report for duty (he never missed a day's rehearsal) but occasionally a bit of extra make-up was needed to cover a black eye or a cut lip from a brawl the night before.

"Alleyn said we were 'armed with many unlawful and offensive weapons.'" Burbage sounded almost hurt by the accusation.

"And were you?"

"I might have had my tools with me, Tom. You know that a workman never goes anywhere without them. A few hammers and axes. But I could see how someone might get the wrong end of the stick," he added with a wink.

"Anyway," he continued, "each piece of timber had to be carefully numbered so that it could be reassembled quickly. Street worked with a close-knit team of trusted craftsmen. They knew once the theft had been detected, suspicion would fall on them, so the materials had to be deployed in the new structure as soon as possible, thereby hiding the evidence. Street arranged for the timber to be stored in a yard, north of the river- close enough to be used to build The Globe and yet hidden from the prying eyes of Allen."

"Wasn't he beside himself, when he found out?" In his mind, Tom could see the mean-spirited leaseholder returning to find that his building had apparently vanished.

"Allen was furious, as you can imagine and tried to sue both of us for theft of his timber and being what he called 'riotous persons.' I was quite hurt by that. I mean, Tom, do I look like a 'riotous' person to you?" He gave his best innocent-looking smile.

Tom looked him up and down and confirmed that no, he did not.

"Three years later, the case had still not been settled and by this time it was like a giant whale on a beach, washed up and spent. The only ones to turn a profit were the lawyers. So, eventually, through gritted teeth, Allen gave up again and here we are. We had to make savings where we could, using ash and nutshell waste from the soap factory along the river to scatter in the yard for example and with a roof of thatch, rather than tile. We couldn't afford the best of everything. All our other material was either still at The Theatre or by now in the failed Blackfriars venture."

"We make use of everything here," chipped in Will. "Objects, word, people- things that others reject, they all wash up here." He stood and looked northwards as if remembering what lay before his eyes before The Globe was built. "Southwark was, and indeed is, a fairly marshy region. We lie here right upon the Thames with its tides and the land is given to flooding. So trenches were dug and filled with 'clunch' which is made from lumps of limestone and topped with oak beams. We even sunk a barrel in the middle of the yard, so that when it rains hard, water drains into the centre. It is like when opinion drifts all in one direction for a reason you cannot explain."

"You seem strangely interested in matters of drainage," commented Burbage.

"I have a stake in this venture, so yes, it is of interest to me if it is flooded or smells as rank as a swamp. Now," he continued, giving Burbage a pointed stare, suggesting a further interruption might not be such a good idea. "The beams were all fitted with mortice and tenon joints and secured with tapered wooden pegs. It was a secure structure but through the course of the summer, the oak would shrink and change shape slightly." He looked around him. "Sometimes, it is like being inside a living, moving creature. Especially at night, it makes strange creaking and howling sounds as if it is almost…breathing." He paused to let the slightly unsettling idea work upon them. "And tell me, Tom, how many sides does this structure have?"

He hadn't really noticed. "Eight?" he guessed. Then he changed his mind. Perhaps it was a trick question and he was being tested. "Perhaps only one- is it round?"

"It looks round from a distance but is not. Sometimes something that looks like one thing from a distance is quite different close up. Jake here, looks like a normal person from far away but on approaching him, you will be aware of the sights and smells that his body produces, few of them pleasant."

He paused for a moment. "It is actually 20-sided." Walking across to the nearest wall, he put a hand up to it. Tom followed his gaze. "The plaster is made from a mix of sand, lime and animal hair."

"Animal…" his voice trailed off. Will nodded. "When they slaughter animals, the soap and glue factories near here try and use every part of them but even they struggle with that, so we made them an offer. The walls are made from wattle and daub and you know what's in the daub? Clay, lime straw, horse-hair and…dung."

"You mean this place is partly made from…that?"

"That's correct. This white plaster seems pristine but the reality beneath- that's what is truly interesting."

He resumed his place with the group. "Take our company, for example. Burbage here takes the main acting roles. Cuthbert," who looked like a slightly older, thinner version of Burbage, "is very much his father's son and has a real business head on his shoulders."

"And you, Will?" asked Burbage playfully. "What is it that you do?"

"I try and write words that will prevent us all from starving."

"And," said Burbage, clapping Will on the back, "he has done an acceptable job of work, so far, would you not say?"

"Aye," came the cry back from the group.

"So, here we are, Tom," continued Will, lighting a small clay pipe. "Beyond the city's jurisdiction, along with the brothels and bear-baiting pits. And that's how the Puritans see us."

"Is there not a risk of fire?" asked Tom, harking back a little anxiously to the detail about thatch. His mother had brought him up to be curious but also cautious.

"I promise to be careful," replied Will, adopting a pose of a naughty schoolboy, looking guiltily at his humble pipe.

"No, I mean with the playhouse and the straw roof."

Will smiled. "I know. Twas but a jest, Tom. But what is life without risk? Anyway, that is how we come to be where we are. Players, part-owners, money-men as well as players. Our fortunes stand or fall not just by our art but by our commerce. Maybe you see now why I worry so over the lines, Tom. They must work hard for us."

"Is that true? Burbage's story about stealing the playhouse."

Will just smiled. "All stories are true, Tom. At least the good ones are. Still, it is time for us to retire. We have much to do tomorrow." In the time that they had been talking, the light had faded and it was really quite gloomy. They got up and started to gather their things together. "Here, Thomas."

The boy turned at the sound of Will's voice. "What?"

"Something for your trouble." He tossed a coin in Tom's direction, which he caught. It was a shilling. Not a fortune but definitely more than he'd seen in a long time. "Get yourself some half decent clothes and come back tomorrow." Rehearsals start at 9 sharp. Don't be late. You're one of us now."

It was dark before he left and the market had packed up and gone. Of Jack and the other cutpurses, there was no sign. Gratefully, Tom quickly scurried home.

As he fell asleep, the face of the chained bear came back to him, forlorn yet defiant, its eyes glazed over with dreams of faraway, snow-capped mountains.

Chapter Three

Tom learns to be both
a hunter and a gatherer

'This wooden O'
(*Henry V*, Prologue, l. 13)

Tom made his way to The Globe with a spring in his step. He dodged the occasional privy pot being emptied out of windows from overhead onto the street below. His mother had taught him from an early age about the awfulness of what she called, 'catching a shower'. If you were lucky it was just stale urine; if not, it was something a lot worse.

Some streets were cobbled, producing a clatter when horses or carts rode over them but with little in the way of drainage, thoroughfares even in towns often resembled muddy country lanes, except what people were walking through was not only mud.

Tom made sure he cleaned his shoes as best he could. He did not need to be nagged about this. His footwear was neither particularly fashionable nor of the highest quality but it was leather at least and with care, could keep out the liquids through which he squelched his way most days.

He reached the playhouse and greeted Cuthbert with a smile but got just a business-like nod in return. It would probably be easier once he had got to know the group. There were about 10-15 members of the main company but they each performed so many different roles and were forever on their way to or from somewhere, it took Tom several days to work out who was who. Initially, he was placed with the apprentice boys who were a bit of a rough bunch but friendly enough. They were mostly younger than he was and liked to tell tales of the scrapes they got into when they were allowed free rein with the beer. That he could believe.

Burbage's brother, Cuthbert, was in charge of 'mysteries of the stage,' which had to remain a mystery to Tom until he had mastered the basics. Outside the playhouse, there was a gulf between some of the company in terms of age, ability and social class. Inside the playhouse, they were all treated as equals. That was all apart from the apprentices who were the youngest members of the company and still learning the trade.

He found himself watching the ginger-headed figure of Ned, who seemed to have complete control of all matters backstage. He was an apprentice too but had enough experience to rank as a manager of sorts of the younger boys who ran about the place like unruly pups. Ned was an energetic figure with a slightly twisted leg and one arm, which he carried as if it was in a sling. Tom knew not to stare and besides such sights were commonplace on the streets.

What was wonderful about Ned though was that from the very first words they exchanged, he was always bright, cheery and helpful. There must have been days when he too was tired and especially annoyed with the apprentices, but he didn't show it.

The boys, most of whom were around 10 years of age, were expected to fetch and carry any manner of things as well as undertake the minor parts- fairies, pages and most importantly, all the female parts. This was a bit of a shock. Tom had never really given it much thought before but all the female parts were played by young boys. It was not seen as respectable for a young woman to appear on stage and each acting company had a few young boys skilled in the use of make-up, costume and wigs to create a credible semblance of a woman. Due to the fashion of big, wide skirts, it was actually not that difficult to disguise a male body shape. Hair could be disguised by wigs and faces were covered with make-up. Voices, though- that was more difficult.

Alongside the players, the fabric of the building itself took time, care and skill to keep it looking good. The company was hardly as rich as an Arabian prince and so most jobs involving painting, mending and even elementary carpentry were carried out by themselves as far as possible. Only when their skills were completely overwhelmed as with wood carving, were tradesmen called upon and it clearly was something Will hated to do, preferring to use the expense to make the performances better.

In the morning, they rehearsed and were trained in all the major disciplines of singing, acting, tumbling, clowning and stagecraft (although Tom wasn't quite sure what that was yet) and in the afternoon, they took part in performances. Ned kept a fatherly eye over this bunch and administered a harsh word and a clip round the ear when necessary. He was not a tyrant but he knew what he was saying and could choose to leave a pin in a costume if someone needed reminding.

No-one sat down and claimed a particular task was 'not his job.' Everybody had to help with everything, with many players taking multiple acting roles in the same production. Like a skilful juggler, this was also something that Will had to consider when writing and very occasionally there would be a howl from a back room, where he sometimes scribbled right up to the last minute, as he realised the same person was needed in the same scene for two different characters. This was a fairly rare occurrence however.

Tom gradually got to know people. On the stage rehearsing at that precise moment was William Sly who was known as 'William' partly to distinguish him from Will and partly because 'Sly' did not sound very complimentary. According to Ned, he often played gallants, dressed in elaborate suits decorated with pearls, sporting a fashionable watch on a chain, waving a handkerchief and doffing his feathered hat to any ladies he found attractive. Sometimes the hero, sometimes the butt of jokes, he would be Paris the lover in *Romeo and Juliet* or the foolish courtier Osric in *Hamlet*.

Will came over to check on progress. "Tell me," he whispered over Tom's shoulder. "What is your real name?"

"Shakespeare."

"No, no. Your real name. Do not worry, you are not in trouble. But just from a practical point of view, it could get confusing having two Shakespeares in the company."

"Swann."

"Ah, a good English name."

"I suppose I should have the courage to use my own name and not hide behind that of another."

Will smiled. "Most people have no say in the names they have. They owe much of their life, for better or worse, to their families and their parents. Perhaps the truest names are the ones we take for ourselves. Well, Thomas Swann, I have a job for you. One to which you are well-suited."

"Me? But I-"

"-Don't worry. Take this page, stand over there and if any of the players forget their lines, just read a few words out loud until they remember. Do you think you can do that?"

"I think so."

So began his first rehearsal. At the moment they were reviving three previous successes, *Hamlet*, *Romeo and Juliet* and *As You Like It* as well as preparing a new play, *Macbeth*. Tom's mother was always telling him how important words were. He did what he was told but until now he'd never really needed to be able to read. Normally, he worked in the fields just outside the city in the summer, threshing corn, which was hard, tiring work and made his hands soon feel like leather gloves. In winter, he begged on the streets of the capital as best he could. Harvest had been so poor that he had been forced to beg all year round. Sometimes they had enough to buy a little food; often they did not.

Despite the immense pressure on everybody to make a play ready, the greatest burden fell on Will, who in addition to his role as an actor and part owner of the company, had to write at least two plays a year as well as make changes to existing plays as the need arose. It was like watching words flow from a spring and it was not surprising that sometimes the spring dried up a little. Indeed, Tom wondered at the toll this was taking on him, considering he also had a whole life back in Stratford about which he rarely spoke.

The pronunciation of some words seemed strange. Tom could read but this was not like the Bible verses he had learned at home and he stumbled over some parts.

"Take your time," encouraged Ned. "Deep breaths- let the words flow through you."

He did as he was told and it helped a bit but he still had a mountain of questions afterwards. Ned patiently explained the meanings of all the unfamiliar words.

"I feel so stupid. All these words and I never knew them."

"Don't feel bad," said Ned. "They are new to most of us as well."

"Are they so unusual then?"

"Oh, very. Will made several of them up".

Tom wasn't sure he'd heard properly. "He…made them up?"

"Oh, yes. He does that quite a lot."

"Are you…allowed to do that?"

Ned threw back his head and laughed. "This is a playhouse, Tom. That's what we do- play."

Later, Tom was in one of the backrooms, carefully doing some copying when Ned's shock of ginger hair appeared over his shoulder. "Don't let the others see that."

"My script is not orderly enough?"

"No. It is your hand. The one holding the quill. You are sinister. That's what they call people who write with their left hand. Who taught you?"

"My mother. She said it was a way to keep me out of trouble."

"Well," said Ned. "That wasn't entirely successful now, was it?"

"What do you mean?"

"Well, you're here, aren't you? Anyway, come and watch the performance."

This was *Hamlet* with Burbage in the title role. At the back of the stage, players entered or exited via a pair of doors, to the right and left of the main stage, and between them stood the tiring-house, covered by a drape. This created a space that could be used for characters to hide or eavesdrop one another, like the busybody advisor Polonius listening to Hamlet and also allowed costumes to be quickly changed and well-placed props to be grabbed. It also provided a spot for Tom to watch and learn. The gallery above the stage could be used for musicians, particularly rich spectators who could pay more to be part of the stage itself (in one of the so-called 'gentlemen's rooms') or it could be used as part of the play, such as the balcony that Romeo must climb up to profess his love for Juliet.

Above the back part of the stage, there was a little shelter from the elements for the players, provided by the so-called 'hut and the heavens'. This was a roof area that extended out as far as two pillars, the underside of which (the heavens) was elaborately painted to represent the stars and the gods beyond. Above this roof lay a little storage area (the hut). In this, props, costumes and even players could be stowed and brought down before a performance or, in the case of players, winched down through a trap if it was necessary for someone to represent a god or supernatural being. Ned had told him about Puck, the mischievous sprite in a *Midsummer Night's Dream*. Supporting the heavens and providing some protection from the weather were two pillars, which stood out onto the middle of the stage. Though made of wood, like most of the fabric of The Globe, they were elaborately painted to give them the appearance of marble and there was such attention to detail in the paintwork, the wooden carving and the general purposefulness of the whole construction, that Tom found it truly a place of wonder.

Ned was himself a tireman. This, Tom learned later, was a term used to describe those who helped with the costumes in the tiring-house. This meant not just the construction or the mending as buttons flew off or seams burst but actually putting costumes onto players who needed help with some of the more elaborate creations.

Tom was just settling down on a stool backstage, when Ned grabbed his arm.

"Look out there," he said, pointing. "What do you see? And I mean really look."

Tom stepped forward and peered out.

The galleries were three stories high and each one was three to four seats deep. Under a short thatched roof and seated on a cushion for an extra penny, the richer members of the audience had quite a different experience of the performance, looking down upon the stage as if gods themselves. Indeed, the arrogance of some was extreme and Ned told him tales of young drunken noblemen who demanded, for a further charge, to be allowed to sit on the stage itself and comment upon the performance as they saw fit. Clearly, in full view of the audience, this was very tempting for babbling idiots who wanted to be looked at and was extremely frustrating for the players who had to put up with constant interruptions. Tom had heard of such business and other places tolerated the practice but here, for some reason, they did not. Perhaps Will was too forceful or too successful to be contradicted. Either way, nobles had to be content to hurl abuse and sometimes the occasional apple-core from the yard like the groundlings.

Those taking their seats in the galleries were clearly of a different class. The men wore silk and velvet in fashionable colours, gold and purple especially, starched ruffs and elaborate hats. Now that they were seated, Tom could not see their lower bodies but most wore doublet and hose, usually with a sword as playhouses were known as rough places. A clearly-visible weapon acted as a deterrent against any would-be robber.

The very few women that there were wore elaborate collars but with a large open neck to display jewellery. Some wore veils and as they were assuming their seats, Tom had noticed rosaries hanging from their waists and huge flared skirts or farthingales as they were known.

He noticed one particular single woman in the galleries. She was accompanied by a male servant to signal that his mistress was respectable and should not be addressed without invitation. She held a fan which she waved from time to time, partly to keep cool in the heat, partly to signal her social status but most importantly, to keep foul odours rising from the yard at bay.

From his life on the streets, Tom usually only saw such figures at a distance. Like any lady considered to be beautiful, her skin was pale, whitened artificially by a mixture of bleaches and mysterious compounds of borax, sulphur and even lead. Ned said such women sometimes suffered bouts of scurvy as a result of choosing to cut vegetables from their diet, which they thought were only for the poor.

The stage from where he was looking was some five feet above the yard, so he could only really see faces and upper bodies but there were certainly lots of them. The groundlings were packed in and already a few scuffles had broken out. Several scruffy-looking boys were hawking their wares, mostly bread or a few had small wooden tankards of ale for the groundlings and stronger Spanish wine or sack as it was known for the nobles in the galleries. The play hadn't even begun and a cloud of steam was already rising from the body of men. You could see why they called them 'stinkards' too with several chewing what appeared to be garlic. There were actually a couple of women in there, including 'apple-wives' selling fruit but from what he could see, there were others who were not exactly respectable, whispering into the ears of half-drunken men, offering a range of dubious services at a price.

Unnoticed at first, Will appeared like an apparition alongside them at the curtain, also known as a 'traverse.' "All the world is here," he whispered. "There are elegant merchants and courtiers in their finest robes down to the poorest labourers virtually in rags. But in terms of their souls- these are much the same and it is our job to remind people of that. However important or rich they are, everyone comes in and leaves through the same doors.

"On a bad day, it can be like...oh, what do they call that dreadful game they play where village teams battle to bring an inflated pig's bladder back to their own settlement? There don't seem to be any rules, just lots of fighting."

"Football?"

"That's it. It's like a football match. But with more violence. There are 3,000 people out there. They come from all walks of life but there is one thing they all have in common."

"What?"

"They have come here to be entertained. Some will have miserable lives and for the two hours of the play, they can perhaps forget some of their woes as they watch stories where someone is suffering worse than they are. They can travel through space and time to places they could never possibly go. They can live as Kings, experience the thoughts and feelings of tragic heroes or comic fools and then at the end return to their daily lives...refreshed. That is our hope anyway. If they don't like it, you might get a few apple-cores thrown at you. If you're lucky."

"How is that lucky?"

"Well, it hurts less than an uneaten apple. And if that doesn't work…"

"Yes?"

"Then there is always music, dance, songs, a few fights and possibly, while they least expect it, an idea."

"An idea?"

He nodded. "Perhaps in the middle of a battle or a dumb-show, a character will do or say something which someone in the audience will not immediately understand but it will stay lodged in their brain like a seed and over time it may take root and…grow." Sometimes Will's images were startling in their originality but at other times, it seemed to Tom, they needed a bit of work.

"Oh, I nearly forgot, since you can read, make yourself useful. Stand there and hold this." He stuffed some pages into Tom's hand. Call out the next few words if they ask for help. "But," he added with a stern stare, "You must wait. If they don't ask for a prompt, you don't give one. Understood?"

There was a world of difference between helping in rehearsal and actually taking that role during a real two-hour performance and Tom turned pale but nodded.

The words he knew were mostly from The Bible, which was the only book he had read. He had grown up surrounded by the stories from the Bible, so the idea of telling stories was familiar but what he had to work with here was completely different. Will wrote on parchment in a grand swirling style and it took Tom a while to connect the words on paper with the lines the players were saying. Luckily, they knew their lines fairly well so at first he didn't have to read anything aloud. He could just listen to the sound of the language, which was like music from an instrument the like of which he'd never heard before. Some of the individual words he didn't know and he was lost for a moment or two but elsewhere a turn of phrase or an expression stuck in his head like a nugget of gold in a muddy stream.

He watched as the stage was littered with bodies until by the end he had lost count how many. He turned back to Ned who was by his side, also watching through the drapes. "Isn't some of this a bit… disturbing?"

Ned flexed his shrivelled arm a little, which ached if he sat too long in one position. "In *Titus Andronicus*, Chiron and Demetrius are murdered, put in a pie and fed to their mother who eats it without knowing."

Tom's jaw dropped open. "And they let children see this?"

"Well, we don't have many children in the audience but some, yes. And of course the apprentice boys who are creating this drama are only about 10. It's best to follow Will's advice."

"What's that?"

"Watch and learn."

The next day followed the same pattern with rehearsal and training in the morning and a performance in the afternoon.

Will had been keeping a sharp eye on the company's newest member and seemed pleased with what he had seen so far. "Tell me Tom," he asked from his desk in the corner of the tiring-house, "what do you need to be a player?"

Tom paused in his reading of that day's play. He spent a good part of the day reading, making himself familiar not just with the words but the problems that would need to be solved on-stage and behind the traverse where they were now. He thought for a moment. "A good memory?"

"That's a start but there is more to it than that." Tom's expression suggested he didn't think there was much more. His mother had warned him to stay away from the playhouse and although he'd often been tempted to sneak in, he was also an obedient son.

"Learning is very important."

Tom was not convinced. What little he knew of school, it was tedious and did little to prepare you for life. Latin and rhetoric- when was he ever going to use such things?

"Did you go to school, Will?"

The older man nodded as if distracted by some childhood memory that wasn't altogether positive. "My mother used to scrub my face before I went to school- 'my morning face' she would call it."

Tom gave a 'Humph' noise, suggesting a distinct lack of enthusiasm.

Will thought of his own experience in Stratford, where he had to be at his desk at seven and work until five, six days a week. It had taught him Latin. He should be grateful for that at least and especially discovering Ovid's poetry and Seneca's tragedies, which had fired his imagination but he had also spent a lot of his time staring longingly out of the window. His dreaminess was often harshly punished and like any other normal boy, he was beaten in school and sometimes at home. He was glad to escape at 15, although this meant he could not go to university and his early marriage barred him from an apprenticeship.

"Books are important, Tom. You have seen me reading and your mother was right to teach you. But there is much more to learn than between the covers of a book."

"You mean going to university?"

Will smiled. "I didn't actually, no. But that can be a noble course of life too. No, I was speaking of something else. As I grew up, I used to spend many hours in the fields and countryside around my home. The trees and plants, birds and other animals- these were my teachers. You can learn a great deal just by watching and listening.

"I used to see the Mysteries being acted when travelling players came to Stratford or indeed on rare occasions when we went to Coventry. The Creation, The Fall, The Flood- these basic stories played an important part in my imaginative life.

"There are many ways to gain an education, Tom. To be a good player, you need lightening-sharp wits for when someone else forgets their lines. You need to be resourceful for when some idiot in the crowd shouts something out but more than that, more than all of that, you need to have a soul."

"A soul?" repeated Tom. His mother made him read the Bible and they went to church when they could and obviously he prayed before going to sleep at night but…soul? He wasn't sure about that.

Will fixed him with his jet-black eyes. "You must possess the soul of a character. You must put yourself in the soul of a character. For if you cannot, how can you expect a crowd to do likewise. Can you do that, Tom?"

He wasn't sure. All this talk of souls sounded like witchcraft and he had been brought up to have nothing to do with that. "My mother says-"

"-Now, Tom," interrupted Will. "I'm sure you respect your mother. And," he added, throwing a disapproving glance towards the company who were enjoying a raucous joke onstage, "that is a good thing. But listen to me and listen well. Once you step through the door of this playhouse, you are your own man, understand. You make up your own mind about things. You speak your mind, explain your ideas and stand or fall by what you say and do but your thoughts-" Here he tapped his forehead. "-These must be yours and yours alone. Understood?"

Tom nodded, although he was still thinking about the words Will had just spoken.

"How old are you?"

"Er, 13, my Lord."

"Right. Well, first things. There'll be no 'My Lording' here. We are different in age, in experience and in material wealth but in this playhouse, we are all equal. And before you get too carried away, that means you do a man's work. No more but also no less. You must work like you've never worked before. You must sweat, you must work till your bones ache. You must bleed if you have to. So can you bear this burden, Tom? Can you be a player?"

There was a long pause. Tom hardly had any choice. He wasn't sure about talk of bleeding but if he went back outside, the gangs would never accept him now and Jack would want revenge for that punch. "I believe, I can, s-"

"-Have we a snake in our midst?" asked Will, provoking some more laughter from Ned. "Well, Tom Swann, I pride myself on being a good judge of character and you…you have something. I'm not sure exactly what yet. But you have qualities. It will be our task to find out exactly what they are. Now, run along and help Gough with the pillars." They had become a little scratched over time and needed repainting. "And see that the stage is properly swept on your way."

The role of prompter involved him with every word spoken by every character and he quickly got to know the plays well. He also learned how to be a 'gatherer,' taking money from people at the door. Even this was not as easy as it seemed. There was a fair bit of pushing and Will had warned him that they had caught previous gatherers pocketing money for themselves rather than putting it straight in the strong-box. The box itself needed to stand safely within the playhouse, so that gangs could not grab it off the street. And Tom also had to swap boxes halfway so that there wasn't so much money in one place to tempt thieves.

Tom was passing through the tiring-house on his way to the main door, when Will called out, "And remember Tom, it's a penny for the yard and a penny more for the galleries and a penny more for a cushion. Got that?"

Tom nodded. "It doesn't seem a lot."

"A penny isn't a great sum- until you don't have it." He looked out at the sea of eager faces who were gathering for that afternoon's performance. "How they even afford that penny is anyone's guess."

"What do you mean?"

"Well, as you know, we must play in the daytime and yet many of these people should be at work now. They are taking the risk of losing their jobs to be here. The job that might keep their family alive. A penny buys a loaf of bread and that's the choice some of these people are making. They'd rather have a full spirit than a full belly. And yet- these plays they have something, something they need more than money."

"And what is that?"

Will and Tom stood at the traverse looking out at the rapidly-filling crowd. "Why do men struggle to plough? Or build new houses? We work to live, yes but once we have some little food in our belly, we need more than the beasts of the field. There is something in our nature that cries out for expression. Call it heart or soul but something. We are not sleepwalking- it is at times like this that we are fully awake." He paused in thought for a moment before adding, "Oh, and keep an eye out for cutpurses."

"Where?" cried Tom, louder than he meant, a little panic creeping into his voice that his place of safety had been discovered.

"No," said Will, lowering his voice, surprised at Tom's flighty reaction. "I mean, keep a good look out during the performance."

"Amongst the groundlings?"

"Mainly, yes but we've had trouble before with thieves dressing as gentlemen so they can worm their way into the galleries where there are richer pickings to be had."

"I'll do my best," Tom promised.

Will took a sober look at the newest member of the company. "Yes, I think you will."

In the brief pause between rehearsal and performance, Tom went to a small plot, not far from the playhouse and also outside the city walls, at the corner of Redcross Street, known locally as Cross Bones. It was only a pauper's grave with little to mark the spot. There had been three Swanns at one point, all boys, but there had been an outbreak of sweating sickness last year and his brothers had both died within a couple of days. Their smaller plots lay next to his father. Tom wondered how long it would be before he joined them.

And whose fault was that? Who had abandoned his family to their cruel fate? Who had made his only son beg in the streets and resort to stealing to survive and feed his increasingly-frail mother? He kicked out in a burst of anger at the cheap wooden cross and it wobbled a little. That made him pause. What was he doing? He looked around guiltily but there was no-one in sight. Not for the first time, tears welled up but this time he let them fall, hot, bitter tears than fell upon the meagre flowers that he had picked from the fields beyond the city walls and lay upon the spot.

He brought his breathing back under control and slowly, the tears stopped, replaced by a steely resolution. He would work hard at the playhouse, no matter what the obstacles were and make his father proud.

When he came back, he was greeted by Cuthbert who fired a question at him. "Do we have enough handbills?" Tom pointed at two large piles on the stage, weighed in place by two of Heminges' tankards. He certainly liked his ale but his drinking did have some uses. They, the bills, would be pressed into the hands of passers-by, making sure they knew that a performance was happening.

"And you have hung out the banner?" Tom nodded. The banner, unfurled from the highest point on the building would let people know from a distance than a play was on that day. "And the fanfare?" Tom had been practising- he had mastered the basics of a trumpet and would be ready to deliver the distinctive call of three loud blasts to play-goers that a performance was about to start.

"Here." Will stuffed a piece of rough paper into Tom's hand as he passed.

"What is it?"

Will turned as he made his way up to the levels above the tiring-house. He was concerned about a problem with moths, which seemed to be feasting on some of his best costumes. "Your next job."

Tom looked down. He scanned the lines which seemed to be spoken by someone called an Apothecary. This was not a prompting job. This was a part. He was about to become a player.

Chapter Four

A Tale of Star-crossed Lovers

'Our remedies oft in ourselves do lie,
Which we ascribe to Heaven.'
(*All's Well That Ends Well* I, (i), l. 231-232)

The next day, Tom resolved to get some extra practice so headed off for 'work,' as he now thought of it, as soon as it was light. As usual, he had to keep his wits about him to avoid being run down by carts, horses and not be swept along by the flood of people all pouring into the narrow streets.

He met up with Will who had come from his lodgings on Silver Street in Cripplegate and together, they approached the Medieval, stone edifice of London Bridge, the only crossing point.

The bridge was teeming with life and the noise was deafening. Merchants, shops, dwellings all competed for interest from the crowds that poured through it, making it seem more like a small town. The many arches beneath made the progress of the largest ships impossible but smaller vessels hastened to and fro. In comparison to Bankside, it was frequented by a better class of customer- one with fewer diseases and more money.

The poorest travelled on foot while gentlemen crossed the bridge on horseback. There were always idiotic drunk men who boasted they could swim across and who dived in, never to be heard of again. Down below, Tom spied several wherries, small rowing vessels, transporting nobles and those able to pay for the privilege across the river, free from mixing with the crowds. These small boats were steered by two to four so-called 'watermen,' sturdily-built figures who skilfully negotiated the fast-moving river and correctly calculated how far they would be carried downstream as they crossed, taking care at the same time to avoid the large coal barges that ploughed up and down the river.

Reaching Bankside, they paused for a moment by a small, temporary stage upon which a group of travelling players were rehearsing a morality play to be performed later in the day. The performances seemed crude compared to what Tom had seen in The Globe but he found himself being drawn in by the fellow playing Adam as he retold the tale of his temptation at the hand of Eve.

Will smiled. "They remind me of my youth a little. Groups of travelling players used to perform mysteries in the town. It was my first real taste of this life. Then I saw The Queen's Men in 1587 when they came to Stratford and I remember they had a wonderful clown called Tarlton, Richard Tarlton. He held us spellbound. It was like another world. Well, it was. But come now, we must press on or we shall be late. He was like the Armin of his age," continued Will as they walked on. "Such incredible energy. And I soon resolved to follow my ambition and become such a player. That's when I-"

He broke off as they turned a corner. Just outside the playhouse, there was a man dressed in a black robe, standing on an upturned crate to give him a position above that of the small crowd who had paused in their business, drawn by the power in his voice. His expression was grave and so were his words.

"Behold," he cried, pointing directly at The Globe. "The sinful nature of the place. Drinking, lechery, thieving- a greater collection of God-forsaken sinners would be hard to imagine. Girls throwing themselves at men, men drinking themselves senseless, cutpurses stealing from the rich, the rich on their fancy cushions up in the gallery imagining themselves better than the groundlings standing below in the pit. And all of them eating, drinking, swearing, shouting- it is like a vision of the deepest pit of Hell!" His voice rose to a crescendo.

"And look there," he pointed. "There is the chief architect of it all." All eyes turned to the figure of Will who had been hoping to creep in unnoticed. He froze, turned and raised his hat to the preacher. "What say you, Mr Shakespeare? Will you repent for your sins? These…plays are a distraction."

"I agree."

The man was shocked into silence momentarily. "I, er, I am glad you share our view."

"Yes, they are a distraction from the lives of misery that many of them live. In perpetual fear of starvation from greedy landlords or damnation from the stories told by ignorant priests." The final two words caused the self-satisfied smile to fall from the preacher's face. "And by what authority do you question our right to advise and help our parishioners?"

"Is that what you call it? Help?" His voice had risen to a pitch that Tom had not heard before and there was a rasping edge to it.

"These plays are a distraction from the life of the spirit."

"I serve the life of the spirit but I do so through a life lived to the fullest." Will turned on his heel, leaving the man open-mouthed before he could think of a reply.

Tom was shocked by the exchange. What the preacher had described as immoral and sinful, Tom had experienced quite differently. It was sheer life! People doing what people do. And were they so evil? Certainly some were doing things they shouldn't but that was why they were there. To play. And what was life without play?

Since falling in amongst theatrical folk, he had been met by nothing more than friendliness and open-heartedness. Well, apart from Jake but then he was unfriendly to everyone. He had never felt so at home. They were his family now.

He had been brought up as a God-fearing boy and before his mother had fallen ill, they would read The Bible together and sometimes even go to Church. He had been taught to respect his elders and betters, especially members of the clergy but these words were so much at odds with his own experience. If the Church was wrong about this, perhaps there were other things about which they were wrong. It troubled him but he followed Will on towards the main door, picking up his feet as he didn't want to be late.

The Apothecary was a fairly small part- he only appeared in one scene and had one main job to do- to sell Romeo a deadly poison. Tom thought it was a part he could do. He could memorise lines. He could deliver them at a pace and volume that the audience could hear. Now whether he could act, only time would tell. Burbage was the leading player of the company but by now he was a little old to play Romeo, so Gough was chosen for the part, meaning he and Tom spent some time practising lines together.

Gough had been a child actor with the Lord Chamberlain's Men before they became The King's Men, so he was a useful source of help for all the questions Tom had. He was young, handsome and typically cast in the role of young lover- like Lysander in *Midsummer Night's Dream* and Romeo in *Romeo and Juliet*. Ned was helpful but he was often busy and Tom didn't want to be bothering him all the time. Gough was more relaxed and knew the business well. However, he did admit to one problem. Although he'd been part of playhouse life since he was a boy, he still struggled to learn lines. Tom, whose own memory was very good, tried different ways to help with this, encouraging Gough to write out the lines, practise them aloud and even have others read them to him while he slept. Nothing worked.

Eventually, Tom had one final idea. "What if you sing them?"

"Sing them? Won't the audience think that's strange?"

"Not in performance," replied Tom, trying to stifle a laugh. "I mean as a way to help you learn them. Sing them to yourself as you go about your day's business. Plenty of them have a musical quality."

That was strange but true and somehow it worked. Admittedly, Gough had several objects thrown at his head from those closest to him who wished he would desist with that infernal humming but it seemed to work and Gough no longer needed to call for help from the prompter.

Performances usually ended with the whole cast going back out to receive the applause of the crowd and a traditional jig, led by the chief clown, Armin, supported by all the musicians and, on a good day, even the crowd joined in.

After the crowd had left and they had tidied up, the company met for some food and a chance to discuss what went right or wrong with the performance. Apprentices were routinely sent out for food and ale or new supplies of ink, quills and paper.

Armin was about the same age as Will but with a shorter beard, shoulder-length hair and a more wrinkled forehead that suggested he was worried, even when he wasn't. He was the energetic soul of the company, letting some of the younger apprentice boys ride around on his back, singing songs or telling stories, accompanied by his ever-present drum.

"When are you going to write some more comedies, Will?" he complained. "I like playing the Fool, you know I do but where is the next *Midsummer Night's Dream* or *Twelfth Night*?"

"Forgive me, Armin but my soul is tainted with darker thoughts these days. Summer turns to autumn. It is the way of things."

"A bit of autumnal sunshine might be nice," grumbled Armin to himself.

"The jig's just good business," explained Cuthbert to Tom. "The crowds go away happy and so even if the play was not to their liking or poorly-performed, their memory is a good one and they are more likely to come again. Don't underestimate how important that is. We live as on the edge of a knife, Tom."

"Even after a successful performance like today?"

"Perhaps especially after days like today."

"What do you mean?"

"No-one wants to live near a playhouse. I admit they can be noisy-well some of the crowd can be, certainly but then so can a bell-ringing church. And we do not make noise during the hours of darkness. The Puritans complain constantly to The Privy Council." The Puritans were extreme Protestants who wanted to wipe out any traces of Catholicism and hated those who devoted their lives to pleasure or luxury, both of which were sinful in their eyes. The man that Tom and Will had seen ranting outside the playhouse was a Puritan.

"What do they complain about?" asked Tom.

"Anything they can think of. They hate us. They hate what we represent. We mustn't give them just cause."

"But why?"

Cuthbert stopped looking through his check-list. He was often to be seen with a piece of paper in hand with certain items crossed out. If you were lucky, you were not one of his items still to be done. "The Puritans hate the playhouses because they see them as places of sin and godlessness. Which, to be honest, they are quite a lot of the time. The Lord Mayor hates them because they take people away from their work, both the players and the audience and puts them in close proximity to one another in an area of the city beyond their power. The more popular we become, the greater grows their fear. For many people, to act is not a reputable profession. Or indeed a profession at all. Religious plays are performed largely without payment. The idea that players should dare to ask for payment seems to some like a kind of trick. They see us as 'masterless men,' people without a legitimate trade. For them, players are basically beggars by another name.

"We survive by a combination of good luck and being liked by certain people- the King especially. As long as we can carry royal favour, the Privy Council will not close us. It may seem like we can do what we like, like a jester of old but like a jester, if we push too far, we can be made to pay. With our livelihoods, if not our actual lives."

Tom shuddered. In these uncertain times, it was enough just to be thought a traitor. If ever he found himself in the Tower, he was sure he would confess to anything, rather than face torture.

Between rehearsals in the morning and the afternoon performance, Will allowed the company a short break. Sometimes this was full of manic last-minute costume fixing or line changes but since Tom had joined, things seemed to be a little better organised. It was a warm spring day and already there were some crowds around the bear-pit. Will suggested a brief stroll along by the river, away from the noise.

They walked in silence for a while before Tom blurted out something that had been on his mind. "Are we going to be rich, Will?"

"Is that what you dream of?"

"No," said Tom, with a slight waver in his voice.

Will smiled. "It's alright. I come from humble beginnings too. It's easy to dismiss the value of wealth when you already have it.

Marlowe's father was a cobbler, Jonson's was a bricklayer and my own family, on my father's side anyway, has fairly modest beginnings."

"But at least now you are a rich man."

"I make no money from the plays themselves."

Tom's brow became instantly furrowed. "What do you mean? You wrote them."

"Yes but they belong to the company. The money we have is from the performance. Those pennies you collect at the door- that is our lifeblood. If I had wished to be rich, I would have stuck to poetry. I wrote two long poems a few years ago, *The Rape of Lucrece* and *Venus and Adonis* for a wealthy patron but I do not write to be famous, Tom. Some measure of financial reward might be nice. I have a family to support in Stratford as well as my family of players here and most of the money I earn disappears into the next play. Being a starving artist is relatively easy.

"It's the owners who make the money. Most get half the take and the other half is shared between 'sharers' which might include the owner. The sharers have a say in hiring players, which play to perform and the business of putting a play together but we have been lucky in having Burbage with us. You have seen him as a great actor, which indeed he is but I think when we look back on this time as old men, we will see Burbage, and his father before him, as crucial. Imagine, we could have had William Alleyne as our master.

"As a sharer, I take about 10% of the profits and perhaps that sounds a lot but the costs are so high, there are often no profits." He looked back towards The Globe with a wry smile. "Playhouses are like giant monsters that swallow money as well as making it."

Tom had nodded but hadn't really followed all of what he was being told.

Will paused and turned towards the great river. "You know, Tom, when I worked at The Theatre, I would go for walks at the end of the day and watch the windmills out beyond the city, the archery practice, even women stretching newly-dyed cloth out on what they call 'tenderfolds.'" He paused as if seeing those things he remembered. "Always keep watching. There are extraordinary things happening around you all the time."

"Really?"

He nodded. "They may not look extraordinary but the workings of the human heart show themselves in the smallest of actions. Always listen too. We're not only sitting by an actual river here. One of the reasons I came to London was to sit and listen to the river of words passing by. I had to learn Latin at school but here you hear French, Italian- all the world comes to London. Tell me, why do you think the playhouses must all be outside the city walls?"

"Plague?"

Will nodded. "That is true also. But the main reason, the reason they will not admit, is that they are afraid."

"The King?"

"Not so much his majesty. He appreciates what we do. No, it is the government around him. There are many factions that plot against one another, whether it is over religion or power or both. I fear my good friend Marlowe became involved in such intrigue and paid for it with his life. When large crowds gather to see a play in which an English king is overthrown, it makes certain people…nervous, shall we say."

"Are they afraid of a revolution?"

"Partly. There have been such things but we English, we do not act from pure choler. Our foreign neighbours sometimes find our cool passions worthy of mirth but what these factions fear more than violence is something the playhouse is full of- ideas. When large numbers of people gather here and imagine a world different to their own, might they then not go home and imagine other different worlds?"

"And so they try and close us down?"

Will nodded again. "They complain to The Master of the Revels about the content of the play if it offends particular religions or is in poor taste. Then there are The Puritans of course who would support any opportunity to close us for…moral reasons."

Tom could not understand this. The people he had met there were all fairly upstanding fellows. Alright so a few groundlings tried to pass on items of stolen property but generally the community he had joined was more law-abiding than the street-life that he had left outside.

"Perhaps the performers scare them too," Will admitted. "People pretending to be something they are not, speaking words that no politicians have scripted, boys dressed as girls. But really, it's the crowds," explained Will. "All that drinking, laughing, perhaps even kissing pretty girls- they don't like that."

Tom's frown deepened. "So they don't like fun?"

Will smiled. "That's about the size of it. To them, pleasure is sinful. So playhouses, along with brothels, asylums, prisons and graveyards must lie beyond the city. Factories too, especially the noisy, smelly ones." Tom thought all factories were like that. "Factories connected with the tanning trade or glue making." Tom wrinkled his nose instinctively at the thought. "We are like a factory too."

"It's not that bad, is it?" Tom replied, somewhat aghast. He knew that there was a steam that rose off the groundlings, especially in light rain or on a particularly hot day.

"No, I mean, a playhouse is like a factory of ideas. That is the product we make best. And that is why they hate us. They are the true enemy, Tom. Those who would have us as beasts without reason."

There was a pause as they were both lost in thought for a while.

Eventually, Tom spoke. "They won't win, will they?" he asked, a little fearfully.

"Of course not." Will looked down at the boy and ruffled his hair. "We shall not let them."

They walked on a little further, soon coming upon open countryside. There was no noise, other than that of birdsong. There were some shed-like dwellings out amid the fields but that was mainly for farmers to store their tools. They were not supposed to build within three miles of the city walls but the law was rarely enforced. London was like an unruly child- growing fast and it was still unclear what it would become. Some said there were even 200,000 people living in the ever-expanding mass of humanity but Tom wasn't sure if he believed that.

"Do you think London will ever spread out here?"

"It's hard to imagine. Why would anyone destroy such beauty?" Will glanced up at the position of the sun. Come now, time to head back.

As they turned back to The Globe, Tom glimpsed a figure standing behind a nearby tree and unless he was mistaken, seemed to be following them. He was on the verge of telling Will but when he looked back, the man had gone.

Chapter Five

A Mystery is Solved

'If music be the food of love, play on.'
(*Twelfth Night*, I, (ii), l. 1-3)

"Now, what instruments do you play?" The question was thrown at Tom by Burbage as soon as he set foot in the playhouse the next day as if it was the most natural thing in the world.

"Instruments?" Tom looked around him as if he'd been asked to produce a diamond out of nowhere. "Er, nothing."

"Nothing?" Burbage ran a hand through his beard as if their might be a solution contained within. Tom might have said that he didn't know how to walk or breathe. "Oh dear, well we'll have to fix that. Heminges!" He called out to John who was taking basic tumbling instruction in the centre of the stage with some apprentices. Although he was somewhat advanced in years, he had been a highly proficient acrobat himself as a younger man and knew the art well. He gave commands about which somersaults to practice and came over to the tiring-house.

"Take young Tom here," instructed Burbage "and give him instruction about an instrument."

Tom had to repeat his humiliating lack of any skill and it produced a similar look of disbelief.

Heminges' generally jolly manner was momentarily knocked back like a cloud passing in front of the sun. "Oh, dear. Anyway, come with me. Let's see what we can find."

Tom followed him up into the musician's gallery and then into the hut above the stage where the instruments were stored. Heminges was a portly man and he puffed a bit in climbing the stairs but for a man approaching 50, he was still full of energy.

"Now, let me see. There's the viol. That's really for dances. Then there's the lute. That's more for love scenes and calming the crowds if too many fights break out. There's the hautboy." Tom wasn't even sure what that was exactly. "That makes a low, haunting sound. Good for the appearance of ghosts or to make the audience feel ill at ease. There's the pipe and tabor but that's quite hard to learn. It looks easy but you have to hold the tabor and stick with one hand. Armin does it while he performs the jig. Then again," added Heminges, "Armin is a bit of a law unto himself." He thought for a moment and then clicked his fingers. His head disappeared into a large chest for a moment before emerging with something that looked like some strange sea creature.

"It is called a bag-pipe and favoured by the Scottish. It is fairly easy to start but hard to produce a serviceable tune. Look, I'll show you." He proceeded to do so for the next half hour, demonstrating the basic finger positioning to create a sound. "But you'll need to practise- at least an hour a day."

Over the following days, Tom did as he was told but the only noise he got from the pipes sounded like a cat being ridden over by a cart.

Will was at his writing table, his head in his hands. "Tom, Tom, TOM!" Will tried to lower his voice. "Do…take a rest. Some folk hold lute music to be almost medicinal, which I can understand. But what you have discovered here, Tom is a sound that would make people ill."

"But-"

"-Yes, I know. You need to practice. But if you keep making that noise, someone will come in here and kill you. And the worst of it is, it could very well be me."

Rehearsal of *Romeo and Juliet* under Will's watchful eye was not going well.

A young apprentice was struggling with the challenging part of

Mercutio. He droned on with little understanding of any of his words. "I see Queen Drab hath been with you-"

"Stop! Stop! STOP!" Will marched over to the poor boy, grabbed him by the shoulders and gave him quite a violent shake. "Queen who?"

"Er, Queen Drab."

"Queen Drab? Queen Drab! The phrase is Queen *Mab*, you…dullard." He released his grip in frustration.

"Oh right," said the boy, nodding. "Makes more sense really."

"Not a lot," muttered another apprentice supposedly helping his mate grind through these lines. Time was tight. Due to illness, the company had been forced to employ some temporary players, many of whom could barely speak, let alone act.

"No, no, NO!" Will's voice rose to a shriek. "Speak the words as I have written them, boy. Do not wave your arms like a windmill in a storm and your face does not need to be pulled in every direction at once. Even the groundlings will laugh at you."

The boy perked up. "That's good, isn't it?"

"NO, IT IS NOT! What I have written for you is not a light piece of comedic flotsam. It is a comment on the nature of our immortal souls."

"Calm down, Will," offered Burbage, trying to ease the situation. "Go easy on the b-"

Will turned and struck him a basilisk stare, almost freezing him to the spot. He turned back to the boy whose smile had vanished. "Now, we will try this again and I warn you, if I do not see some gargantuan improvement, you will be joining the beggars down by river and possibly floating in it. Lifeless and with a large blade sticking out of your neck."

The rehearsal continued and to his credit, the boy found his motivation much improved.

They took a short break, which was to save the boy's life as much as cool Will's temper.

Burbage, the eternal optimist was trying to convince the company that all was well. "He's just a bit nervous, that's all. As soon as the performance starts, he'll be fine."

"FINE?" screamed Will. "FINE?" His temper had not cooled greatly. "We'll be lucky not to be laughed off the stage. He has a speech of great import to deliver and he can barely open his mouth, let alone remember the right words. We are doomed."

A heavy stillness settled over the company.

Eventually a small voice piped up. "Er, I could do it." All eyes turned towards the owner of the voice-Tom. "Well, I know the words and I've watched the boys practising. I could give the sword fights…a try." His voice tailed off.

"A try?" repeated Will. He stood up. Tom expected to feel the blast of his scorn. "That might just work."

Tom opened one eye. He'd screwed up both tight shut, prepared not for the slings and arrows of outrageous fortune but a blow from Will Shakespeare's actual fists. "Yes?"

Will nodded. "But you must promise me, promise us that you will give of your utmost. We will be taking a risk on you."

Tom had seen Will once passing on his way into the playhouse, stop and stare intently at a dice game on the street. He seemed drawn to games of chance but his ever-alert eyes were not those of a natural born gambler. He had sized up the odds and moved on.

Some time later, Will was engrossed in writing and then rewriting as his quill scratched at a piece of parchment. His words had almost disappeared beneath crossing out. He happened to glance up and caught Tom watching him.

"What is it?" he asked, pointing at the words.

"A sonnet."

"A what?"

"A sonnet. A 14-line love poem."

"Why are you writing that?"

"The mind is like a restless dog. It needs to be exercised. Daily. There is a particular way that the lines rhyme and scan." There was a pause. Will could tell there was something troubling him. He put down his quill. "Go on. Holding a question inside is like trying to contain a fever. It just makes the patient worse."

"Well, when I was acting as prompt, there were all kinds of words and phrases I'd never heard before and I thought that was just because well, I'm young. But then I asked Ned and he didn't know any of them either. And then he said he suspected you just…made them up." He tried to think of an example. "In my mind's eye.' Where does that come from?"

"Ah."

"It's not like I am criticising you, er, Mr Shakespeare. You have been very good to me. But I mean, are you allowed to do that?"

Will walked away a little as if trying to find the words to help him understand. "Tom, if something comes into my head and I write it down, what's the worst that will happen? Will the master-at-arms break down the door and have me arrested for crimes against language?" He smiled. "And besides, if the groundlings do not follow an idea, eventually they will stay away."

"But some of these words- they are not even English."

"What of it? Latin is well and good but English, Tom, English is the language of poetry. English is a great thief and always has been. I would have thought you should appreciate that."

"What do you mean?" Tom was never sure exactly how much Will knew or could guess about his life before he entered the playhouse.

"I mean, as a reader, you can see how English has 'stolen' terms from many languages. It is true a few French and Italian items pepper my work like a well-seasoned meal but it is not to make the crowds admire my learning. The richer the palette, the better the painting, my father used to say. The original versions of some of the stories that I have rewritten, *The Merchant of Venice* and *Othello*, the tale of a Moor, for example, can only be read in Italian. I know a little and what I don't know I ask from friends. English is not the only language in the world. Storytelling, now that is a language for all the world.

"What I know, I know from reading yes but more from watching and above all, listening." He paused and held up his hand a moment. "London is like a giant hive. Sometimes all you hear is the general buzz-buzz but listen closer. Observe. Each bee has his own allotted place and time. There is method in it. I just try and find the sweetest flowers and sometimes, just sometimes, make something worthy of them."

53

"But do you think they, the groundlings I mean, really understand all of your grand speeches?"

He shook his head. "It doesn't matter. Those 'grand speeches,' as you call them, are mostly for the folk in the galleries. And not all of them will understand either. Don't ever confuse education with intelligence, Tom. A million years of schooling will not make some of them clever and vice versa. Those figures you see in the pit at the front- they are not without wit. It is always from there that we have the best comments, not from the perfumed courtiers.

"The groundlings come for diversion, for sport and that is what I try and give them. A song, a dance, a fight. Perhaps a love story and a murder of an English King to help people their dreams. When they cheer for Henry V beating the French at Agincourt, their bellies are not rumbling for a couple of hours.

"It matters not what words you know- it's what you do with them that counts. Who is to say what you or I can or cannot say? A word is a thing or an action? If it is understood, it is a word.

"When babes first learn to speak, they oft use words that only their parents understand and brothers and sisters laugh and find it a thing of magic. Why then, when we are older must we cast off this magic and become as colourless as the dullest winter sky? I say we should try and keep this magic."

"But-"

"-But what?"

"But in *Hamlet* for instance, Will. You have dozens, scores of words the like of which I have never heard- 'blinking idiot,' 'foul play,' 'tower of strength.' It's…like a waterfall."

"A good phrase, Tom. Perhaps we'll make a poet of you yet. And you fear the groundlings will drown in this waterfall? Well, I would rather see it as an invigorating shower that will unlock-" Tom's brow furrowed at yet another new word- "the cabinet that holds their imaginations fast. I cannot change. It is all I know. They will follow where I lead them. Do not think the groundlings shallow. It is they who must make a leg of pork last a week. It is they who must keep the crying babe from screaming in hunger. It is they who are most in need of hope. Do not tell me they lack in power of mind."

A different question occurred to Tom. "Why do you not write about here? About London, I mean."

Will threw back his head and laughed. Tom was disconcerted. He hadn't said anything funny. The laugh subsided and Will took a moment to compose himself. "It is a pity, my boy, that you are not a writer of comedies. So I have not written about my circumstances, you say?" He fixed Tom with an intense gaze that seemed to bore into his head. "Not everything is what it seems. We must not upset the Master of the Revels. If it looks like the story is critical of those in power, we may not get a licence. The master is an old man called Tylney, Sir Edmund Tylney. He's been doing the job for...well, it seems like forever. He must be the best part of 70 now. We've had a long understanding with him but it seems he's becoming harder to please. He can demands cuts to lines or scenes that he feels insult the Monarch, the Church or public decency. And without a licence, we can be treated as 'rogues, vagabonds and sturdy beggars.'"

Tom shuddered. This last part he knew all too well. Punishments for vagrancy- sleeping on the street and not having a job to go to- included being whipped out of town and being branded on the right ear.

Will followed his gaze. "I write about what separates us from the beasts. Or, sometimes what does not. Love, greed, hatred, ambition- these are forces that drive our nature just as much here as in Milan or Verona. Do you think when I write of *Henry VI*, people are reminded of the real King? They know next to nothing of history. Do you think when I place Julius Caesar in Rome, anyone is reminded of the time they visited that fair city? We have a scattering of merchants it is true but few in our crowd have any sense of the architecture, the life, the reality of cities like Venice. My Venice has no canals, my Egyptians play billiards and my Julius Caesar has a clock to tell the time." He came closer and put his hand on Tom's shoulder.

The same is true of costumes. I have read some Plutarch but I do not know what people wore in ancient times. Nor do I care. Richard III may not have had a crooked back, a lengthy nose or indeed murdered the princes in the Tower but what is important is that the audience believe such things could be.

"In *A Merchant of Venice* or *Two Gentlemen of Verona*, all the characters speak English rather than Italian and for *Macbeth*, although clearly taking place in Scotland, we shall not be attempting a Scottish accent."

"Why not?"

"Very few people here know what it sounds like. Why instruct players to change their voice, spend many hours practising and to what end? It is like costume."

"I don't understand."

"As you noticed, my plays do not take place in the London of today. Nor tomorrow." Tom chuckled at the idea of stories from the future. "The comedies? Well, they're in a world of their own. Like ours, perhaps even related to it but different. But the histories and tragedies? They often come from the past. Sometimes it is within memory of those still alive but that is a very short time. Mostly, my stories come from a past long departed from memory." He paused, unsure whether he was making himself clear or just confusing the boy. "The costumes that characters wear are very important- sometimes that is the sole reason for some people attending. But I am not interested in whether there is verisimilitude. Whether," he added, seeing Tom's face cloud over at the long word, "the people I write about really did wear such things. I do not know if Macbeth looked as we shall dress him, neither do I care. That is not important. What is important is that he looks like his character as I have written it. He is a great soldier, a saviour of the nation but he is also a nobleman. He owns his own castle and is a trusted advisor to the King. As long as these elements are there, all else is secondary. We have no drawings of the man, no testimony, no witnesses. I am not recording history. I am making history.

"The world of which I write is not the physical world, the here and now. Most people who come here want to escape that. What we create here is but a couple of hours respite from suffering and misery. It is the world of the imagination." He thought for a moment. "Come with me."

He strode out of the tiring-house and across the stage, before leaping down into the yard, Tom scurrying behind, trying to keep up. Without slowing, Will marched out of the main entrance at which point, he turned and pointed upwards. There, high on the outer wall, was a crest with a strong, muscular man carrying the globe on his shoulders. "Recognise him?"

Tom craned his neck upwards. He'd seen some strong men in travelling circuses and this looked a bit like them but he was guessing that wasn't what Will meant. He shook his head.

"Why do you think we have that design?"

Tom stared up. "Well, it's a globe." He looked at Will as if the connection was obvious. "The name of the place."

"Yes, yes, of course but who is the figure and what is he doing?" Will went on to answer his own question. "Usually Atlas carries the Globe but that is Hercules relieving him of this burden for the duration of the play. When people come to see a play, we provide escape, relief even. During this magical time, divisions between men, rich and poor, Protestant and Papist, all different vocations- all are mixed together. This place, this-" he looked around at the circular structure- "...wooden 'O,' in a single day, holds more people than all the citizens of Stratford. For those two hours, we create a new town, a new citizenship. Those few, those happy few, will see and hear things that no-one else ever will- it is a unique once-in-a-lifetime experience. Can you read the words beneath it?"

Tom peered again and read aloud in a halting delivery. "'Totus mundus agit histrionem."

"Does that mean anything to you?" Tom shook his head and blushed in embarrassment. "Don't worry. Not everyone has the benefit of learning Latin. I did not go to university, you know but I have a little schoolboy Latin. It means, 'the whole world is a playhouse.' What do you understand by that?"

Tom thought for a moment. "That all is for mirth only. Nothing is serious."

Will nodded. "Partly. But it also means this world here, within this playhouse can create the entire world. In some legends, gods destroy worlds but we can create them.

"Then we also use different coloured flags to make sure audiences know what they're coming to. Red for history, white for comedy and black for tragedy."

Tom had recently read *Measure For Measure*, which had a bit of everything, and wondered what flag they'd put up then but he kept that thought to himself.

"Why have a flag at all?" he asked.

"Well, we are outside the city and at some distance from where most of our audience live." He pointed northwards. "We need to lure them across the river. You say I do not write of the world around me," he continued, shaking his head. "Precisely the opposite is true. I mean it is only by interrogating it, really pulling it to pieces that you can see how the human form works. He continued. "A good writer absorbs the world around him and makes it new. If I just copy the world as it is, of what interest is that? People want to be raised up, above the animals and this is what we do. After the daily toil, what is there in life? Why do we plough the field, build the church or herd the sheep? To survive? If there is a God, does he not want us to do a little more?"

"So we are doing God's work?"

"In a way, Thomas, we are. Administering to the soul."

Will took the evening off from writing to talk with Tom about the role of Mercutio, who was a strange character- part fool, part braggart, a sensitive, poetic soul but one who eventually ends up being killed because he fights a needless duel.

They talked into the evening and as darkness had fallen, the pair, looking every bit like father and son, walked together towards Tom's home in Cheapside.

Suddenly Will pulled Tom into a doorway out of what meagre light was cast by a sickly-looking moon.

"What the-?" began Tom but Will put a gloved hand over his mouth to silence him.

"There," he whispered, pointing at the street behind them.

"What?" Tom looked but saw nothing.

"THERE," said Will in an exasperated tone. Slowly Tom's eyes adjusted to the light. Or the lack of it. Creeping slowly along the street, keeping largely to the shadows, was a figure, a man as far as he could tell but whose features were covered with a scarf. It was the same man he had spotted down by the river.

Tom opened his mouth to explain this but Will continued. "He's been there since we left the playhouse. Come on, let's see if we can get rid of our unwanted flea." Will stepped out again into the open street and together the two progressed half a mile further, taking a few specific twists and turns to make the way less obvious. Again they dropped into a doorway and waited.

Shortly afterwards, the same figure appeared. He was definitely following them.

Will reluctantly put his hand to the hilt of a dagger that he had begun to carry ever since young Kit Marlowe met his end in a knife fight. He had never had to draw it in self-defence. Until now.

"Quick, Tom. Conceal yourself." They were just passing a tavern and nearby there was a low wall of a stable block still under construction.

They crouched down and waited. Moments later, the man appeared and looked around him, clearly lost.

"Now," cried Will and the pair of them, Will with his dagger drawn, pounced and wrestled the figure to the ground. Surprisingly, he didn't put up much of a struggle but in the darkness of the street, it was impossible to identify him.

"Come," said Will. "Let's see who this is." Between them they manhandled their prisoner towards the only source of light- the tavern

They staggered inside and veered away from the bar where there were a few customers and avoiding gaming tables, they chose a relatively quiet corner. Once seated, one either side of their captive, they whipped off the scarf and Will held the man's face up to the nearest candlelight a little roughly like valuing a prize calf.

At once, Will released his grip and fell back in shock. "You?" He knew the man. He knew him very well indeed. "What are you doing here?"

Tom looked at the stranger and then back at Will. "Who is this?"

"Well," he said, allowing the man to stand on his own two feet. "Tom, may I introduce you to Edmund. Edmund Shakespeare." There was a pause. "My brother."

Chapter Six

A New Recruit

'Why, then the world's mine oyster,
Which I with sword will open.'
(*The Merry Wives of Windsor*, II, (ii), l. 4-5)

There was a pause as Tom tried to take this in. "I did not know you had any brothers." Will rarely talked of his family.

"I have three- Gilbert, Richard and Edmund here- the youngest. 16 years my junior."

Indeed it was hard to believe that Edmund was Will's brother, he looked so much younger. There was more of the son than the brother about him. He looked to be in his twenties and there was a similar intensity in the dark eyes but a softness of other features. His hair was starting to thin on top but was brushed over in an attempt to hide this and his beard looked more like a half-hearted hobby. What set them apart was Edmund's slightly mad expression- his eyes were restlessly looking around as if for some form of escape. Tom felt if they did not keep hold of him, he would run off like a hare slipping out of a trap.

Edmund eventually realised that some sort of explanation was needed. "I have a letter," he stammered and rummaged in his thin jacket. Now that they could see him better, he looked poorly-clothed to be out at night.

"What?"

"A letter. From, well, you will see." He eventually pulled out a crumpled piece of paper and thrust it towards Will, who flattened it out and held it up to the nearest light, struggling to make sense of the scratchy writing.

Dear Mr Shaksper,
I promised your father, who was a good alderman to this town, that I would do my best to help and I have tried to train Edmund as an apprentice in the business but alas, I have met with little success. He is not without ambition but the industry which should attend it. Please do what you can for him.
Yours William Makepeace Esq, Makepeace's Brewery

Post Scriptum: He has some limited ability to read and can figure a little.

Tom just sat, still in shock. Will had a brother, his father was an important figure and was that really how you spelled his name?

Will was concentrating on more important matters. "Edmund, you weren't caught drunk again, were you?"

"No! I just…put the wrong hops in the wrong cask."

"An entire batch?" Edmund nodded reluctantly. Will gave a low whistle. "It is scarcely a surprise then that Makepeace wants rid of you." He sighed. "So what are you doing skulking around here?"

"I just thought…you might be able to help."

"You travel hundreds of miles from Stratford without telling me, just on the chance that I would somehow…weave my magic?" There was an edge of anger in his voice.

"I just thought…" Edmund's words tailed off.

"Yes, that is your problem. You did not think."

"But, can't you just…I mean, you are…Shakespeare." Edmund's words didn't make a lot of sense but his pleading eyes conveyed his meaning well enough.

"Edmund, I did not just wake up one day with crowds cheering my name. I learned this trade over years. Years when I was ignored. Years of hard toil." He had forgotten how exasperating his little brother could be. "I will help you as best I can but you must set your shoulder to the grindstone."

"You sound just like father," muttered Edmund, nettled.

"That is scarcely a surprise." Will's father had died only a few years before. "I am his eldest son. And he was not wrong about everything."

"Anne has spoken of how distant you are."

"Well, London is a good three day's ride from Stratford."

"That was not her meaning. As well you know."

"Thank you for the message, little brother. But I do not need to be told how to treat my wife." His tone softened a little. "Come to the playhouse tomorrow. We'll see if we can find a role for you. Is that acceptable?"

Edmund managed a reluctant nod. He was clearly ecstatic at the thought of working with his older brother whom he had looked up to since birth but there was also plenty of pride in his clenched jawline.

Will put his forefinger to his lips. A gesture that Tom had seen before. It usually heralded an idea. Will nodded to himself as if conducting some kind of discussion and coming to a conclusion. "I may have something for you."

The senior figures in the company were having a slight difference of opinion.

"Tybalt!" shrieked Burbage, his voice rising in disbelief.

"It's perfect, Burbage."

"But...but...he's only just joined the company." Will had announced his brother's new status to the rest of the company at the start of the day and several eyebrows had been raised.

"We must always be on the lookout for new talent."

"And that's Edmund, is it? Sorry, I know you are kin but he is...untested on the stage and seems too...boisterous for this life." Burbage chose his words carefully.

"I know the demands of the playhouse but I also know that we have suffered a number of losses in recent years." Several players had died, leaving the company understaffed. For the number of productions they were expected to undertake, some extra labour could prove very useful. What remained unspoken was whether the loss of several key players, especially their clown Kempe who was an endless source of charismatic energy, had also robbed the company of some of its youthful vigour.

"Edmund has certain…qualities and for the part of Tybalt, he will serve his purpose. All his scenes feature him talking about fighting, wanting to fight or actually fighting. We need a character who picks fights, speaks few lines and thinks he is the best."

At that very moment, the man himself strode into their midst and the conversation stopped. Edmund looked round the group, none of whom would meet his gaze, making the subject of their discussion very obvious.

"Look," continued Will. "He's just a boastful hothead."

"What do you mean?" blurted out Edmund. "I'm the youngest brother of William Shakespeare, the greatest writer in the world!"

Will sighed. "I was talking about the character of Tybalt." There was a pause and then the group burst out laughing and to his credit, Edmund, red-faced, joined in at his own foolishness. "Although you could see how I might have been confused. But you do get to fight."

At that Edmund perked up. "Really?" Will nodded.

"Yes, yes but when do we get to practice the fighting?" asked Edmund in bored impatience.

"Soon enough, young Tybalt," replied an increasingly-exasperated Burbage. He wanted Edmund to at least have some idea about the words he had to say too but to speak truthfully, he did also want Edmund to practice his fight scenes. He was so hot-headed, he might go and kill Mercutio for real, rather than accidentally like in the play.

This also was a concern for Tom since he was now playing the part of Mercutio. He had rather hoped to survive the week at least.

He explained his fears to Will who reacted in a way he did not expect. He laughed.

"Listen Tom, Mercutio is someone who loves to play with words and we need someone who can learn and deliver that Queen Mab speech. He is an outsider. Intelligent, strange, with a certain sadness about him. Who better than you? Besides, it will give you a chance to show your fencing ability."

"What fencing ability?" Tom had never even owned a rapier, let alone used one in a fight.

"You will learn quickly in practising with young Edmund here. Well, either that or he will kill you."

So, it was that Tom practised daily with Edmund, under the watchful blue eyes of Condell who was the company's best swordsman. He did not have the stature of Burbage and his small mouth and soft features seemed almost feminine but there was nothing soft about the way he could wield a sword and he explained the basic moves with precision. This was important as many of the plays involved fights and crowds expected to see something realistic. Tom found himself having to learn the basics of fencing at break-neck speed.

Will watched him practising with a sense of growing horror and held up a hand to pause proceedings. "Where on earth did you learn to fight?"

Tom was forced to explain sheepishly that he had never really handled a sword.

Condell took Will to one side and whispered, "We must find a way that Edmund can somehow learn the basics of swordsmanship without killing other people. Or himself. Any ideas?"

Will had no wish to lose one of their leading players due to Edmund's youthful enthusiasm.

"I do actually, yes."

Chapter Seven
Watching and Learning

'Were it my cue to fight, I should have known it
Without a prompter.'
(*Othello*, I, (ii), l. 82-83)

Early the following Sunday morning, before people left for church, Tom, Edmund and Ned walked northwards up through the city to an area, not far from the former site of The Theatre where Will and several of the others began their acting careers. Edmund was moaning about having to get up so early, how little breakfast he had had and how far he was having to walk. This was especially ridiculous as everywhere was close enough to walk, although they might not have done so at night, when it was pitch black and low-life criminals would prey on anyone foolish enough to be alone. At that moment, Ned was considering taking Edmund out for a night-time walk and then running away.

Just behind the main thoroughfare was a huge, flat open space, rectangular in shape and surrounded on three sides by a low hedge and on this glorious summer morning, they could see even as they approached from a distance, a group of men in this arena, engaged in some very earnest activity. It was here, out in the fields where dozens of noblemen took their regular archery and fencing instruction. Will's usual instruction rang in Tom's ears: 'Watch and learn.'

The three of them crouched behind the hedge and observed as a pompous-looking, little man stood on a box and shouted instructions to a group of about 30 young men, few apparently listening to him.

They were engaged in the much more important business of worrying about their appearance. Each of them was wearing the cleanest, brightest, shiniest clothes Tom had ever seen. Many were practising their stances, others took a few steps forward to parry or dispatch an imaginary opponent but the majority were just standing, preening themselves like prize cockerels, concerned about their hair, the creases in their clothing and whether they were looking their best.

The reason for this demonstration in arrogance became clear when a carriage containing the high peal of female laughter rolled past, stopping briefly to allow some incredibly-expensive hats to emerge. At that point, backs straightened, chests were thrust out and voices, deep before, were made even more deep and manly, almost as if they were seeking to impress the occupants of the carriage.

"I'm going in," said Edmund impulsively.

"What?" cried Ned. "You can't. What if they recognise you?"

"Why would they?"

"Well, your clothes for a start."

"Ah, well I have a plan there." He opened his coat a little to reveal the grand costume of a gallant from their current production. He was literally wearing a fortune.

Ned gasped. "If Will catches you, he'll....I don't know what he'll do but it won't be good for you." There were heavy fines imposed on company members who wore playhouse costume outside the premises.

"Well, then," said Edmund with a wink. "Better make sure he doesn't catch me."

"It's no joke. If you are found out, they could hound you to death. For some, impersonating a gentleman, seeking to step above your position in life- there is no worse crime. Tom, can't you stop him?"

Tom had been watching this exchange with growing alarm. He didn't how he could stop him. Edmund was twice his age and if he set his mind on something, it was nearly impossible to divert his attention.

"Come on, Tom. You can be my servant." Without waiting for an answer, Edmund disappeared through a gap in the hedge and strode confidently over to the men.

"Tom…Tom…don't do this. TOM!" Ned hissed as Tom followed Edmund's bad example and entered the field. Tom didn't think it was a good idea any more than Ned did but he couldn't just stand and watch Edmund be cut to pieces

Edmund made his way to the nearest group and tried casually to blend in. Tom took up a position as close to Edmund as he dare as his 'master' ran through a few drills with his own sword. Luckily for both of them the real focus of attention was either on the progress of the female laughter in the mid-distance or on themselves. They weren't actually that much concerned with one another.

These noblemen, most of whom did little for a living other than spend their family's inherited wealth, usually trained in expensive and exclusive fencing schools, but in the summer months enjoyed the chance to practice in the open air. And if some attractive and admiring young women happened to pass by, well they would just have to do their best to ignore the distraction.

"I have not seen that stroke before," a voice behind Edmund said. "Mr…"

The pause was clearly meant to be filled with a name. Unfortunately in all his planning about costume, Edmund had neglected a rather important part of his role. A name.

Tom, on the other hand, had spent many hours in the tiring-house, watching through the drapes and had observed the noblemen in the galleries- how they dressed, how they moved, even how they greeted one another. He had watched and he had learned. "This," interrupted Tom, "is Lord…Tybalt. I am his page."

"And a very impudent one who dares interrupt his master," snapped the man. "And what kind of…livery do you call that?" He poked somewhat disrespectfully at Tom's rough tunic, which was what he would normally wear for rehearsal. "You look more like a…peasant."

"I humbly beg your pardon," said Tom, sounding genuinely sorry.

Tom furiously nodded towards the ground and eventually Edmund got the hint and turned, delivered a deep bow and addressed his questioner. "Er…Tybalt. Lord Tybalt."

Tom had resorted to the name from *Romeo and Juliet*. Tybalt was the hot-heated member of the Capulet family who wanted to kill Romeo, a Montague, for daring to attend a family party uninvited.

"Tybalt," repeated the man. "That sounds…familiar."

"Ah, yes," said Edmund, grateful for Tom's quick-thinking but unable to match it with any of his own. "I am known in some quarters," he added eventually, "as the King of Cats."

"And why is that?"

"My Lord trades in furs," interrupted Tom again but faced with another furious stare, held his tongue further.

"And," Edmund added nervously, showing his full mental agility. "I like cats."

Tom winced at such a terrible lie but his questioner only seemed to be half-listening and Edmund was soon invited over to meet some other gentlemen.

For his part, Edmund had expected this to be difficult but he found being a gentlemen consisted mainly of wearing the right clothes and assuming everyone was less important than you were. For his part, his new friend noted Edmund's lack of speed of thought and his slightly odd accent which couldn't quite place but he could not argue with his magnificent clothing.

So it was that he was introduced to several other fellows as Lord Tybalt, King of Cats without a murmur of surprise or shock. It seemed once he was accepted by one or two influential individuals, the mass would follow suit.

Ned, watching from a distance, had expected them both to be sliced up within seconds but found himself chuckling in admiration at Edmund's courage. Or stupidity.

Edmund found his attention was also drawn by the female audience and found himself trying slightly harder to make his stance more rigid and his thrusts even more impressive. If he had had to engage in more conversation, he probably would not have been able to maintain the pretence of being a gentleman but luckily all he had to do was act the part, something for which he was finding he had quite a talent.

After going though lots of drills, the time came for some actual combat.

The fencing master said that he had a little piece of business to attend to (Tom suspected it probably involved a drink for it was a hot day) and that he needed to be gone for just a short time but would return shortly. They were reminded about the dangers of such activities and that they should only use blades with caps on the points. With that, the rotund little fellow mopped his sweaty brow with a handkerchief and retired from the field, waddling in the direction of the nearest tavern.

The fencers began sensibly enough. And yet, Tom could feel the rise of youthful enthusiasm amongst some participants at the prospect of genuine combat. It was at that point that he was paired with a new partner. He tried to explain that he was just a page but since they had uneven numbers, it was expected that even servants should match up and join in.

He found himself facing a quintessential gallant. He wore a ridiculous hat with a pink ostrich feather sticking out of it, a huge ruff, a cloak of what looked like satin and other garments covered with elaborate lacework and not a few jewels. He seemed to be dressed more for a visit to the playhouse than fencing but Tom supposed the purpose was the same- to be seen. He had a big bushy moustache, which he insisted on stroking like a pet cat and it seemed almost the same size. Tom felt he half-recognised the man but it was hard to be sure. Noblemen filled the galleries at The Globe but these gallants often looked virtually identical. Only by an even bigger ruff or even more jewels could you distinguish between them.

"Oh, dear," apologised Tom. "I seem to have forgotten my sword. Gloves too, so I'm afraid-"

"-That's no matter. My servant will lend you some." He snapped his fingers and the missing equipment appeared as if by magic.

"Oh...good," said Tom in a tone which suggested the opposite.

"Pembroke," snapped the man, and tapped Tom's sword with his own, as if that was introduction enough.

"Swann," replied Tom, in an equally clipped tone, which sounded ridiculous to his own ears.

"Let's do this buttons off, shall we?"

"I beg your pardon?" said Tom, genuinely not sure what he meant. Pembroke explained by removing the small device at the end of the rapiers, both that he was using and one he had lent to Tom. "No masks?"

"What are you? Some kind of girl?"

"No, I just value my sight."

"You'd better defend it then," blustered Pembroke. "And," he said taking out an expensive-looking moleskin purse, "I suggest a small wager." He picked out a bright, silver coin. "Shall we say a crown? Unless that's too rich for your blood?"

Tom shook his head, having no idea what he'd do if he lost. A crown was worth 60 pennies. The entrance fee of 60 people at The Globe. It was a considerable sum. He had about tuppence on him. Oh, why hadn't he listened to the wise advice of Ned?

"Right, then. Let's give the ladies something to look at, shall we?" he snarled and attacked with a vicious series of lunges that took Tom quite by surprise. Luckily, the hours of practice he'd done with Ned paid off and he managed to parry most of the blows but was forced backwards, stumbled and fell on the dusty ground with a thump.

Pembroke turned to receive the applause of the group, and noted, much to his approval, a squeal of delight from the carriage.

Tom gathered himself again, took a few deep breaths and he it was who attacked this time, forcing his opponent back, scattering the young men, who were starting to revel in what appeared to be a genuine fight.

Pembroke had superior technique- he had been fencing since he was at school, Tom suspected. And yet he was not as fit as once he was and as the fight wore on, a shiny patch of sweat appeared on the man's head. There was a price to be paid for his fashionable appearance.

Tom persevered and attacked again with an Italian sequence of strokes he had only just learned. This wrong-footed Pembroke who was forced backwards. Tom could feel his blood rising. Pembroke was little more than a bully who thought it was good sport to humiliate those weaker than himself.

The older man collected himself, looked around at his male and female admirers who were a little less sure of him now and felt the need to re-establish his position. This…boy was all very well but it was important to keep people like that in their place. He, on the other hand, had been born to have the best things in life and that included winning at games like this.

Edmund watched on helplessly as from his boot Pembroke produced a dagger and turned to face Tom, holding up both weapons.

"Now-" began Tom.

"I hope Mr Swann does not mind a little…extemporisation. Or has the page of the King of Cats lost his nerve?" There was a slight ripple of laughter round the group. The men encircled the fighters now and Tom realised that there was no retreat. He must fight.

He drew a dagger from his own belt. The importance of a sharp knife was also something that he had learned from his time as an aspiring cutpurse. It was a favourite game among the thieves to challenge each other to see if they could cut the purse-strings of a nobleman or lady without making a sound.

The pair slowly circled each other, looking for advantage. The older man made a feint at which Tom staggered back, making the crowd laugh. Tom's cheeks burned red. He had to keep his wits about him. He didn't intend to die that day.

Pembroke made a strike with his sword, which Tom blocked but his opponent's dagger followed just a little too quickly and caught Tom on the arm. Luckily it was only a light wound and to his right arm, not his main sword-carrying arm but it still wasn't good. The hope that he'd had of tiring out the older man on a hot day seemed a faint one if he was despatched quickly himself.

Where he might be better was in matters of speed and agility. Tom tried a lunge with his rapier, which was immediately parried but this brought them close together. His opponent raised his dagger ready to strike but Tom stamped down hard on his instep, causing Pembroke to yelp in pain. It was the sort of move you learned living on the streets rather than in grand houses.

Pembroke continued to cry out. "That, sir, is…ungentlemanly."

"Perhaps so," countered Tom with a tight smile. "But you said to extemporise."

As time went on however, his luck started to turn. Pembroke had been training for years and his technique was better. He knew tricks and short-cuts which Tom did not and above all, he was fuelled by fear at the shame of being beaten in a public combat by a mere servant. Slowly but surely, he began to work his advantage.

All friendly rivalry had disappeared from his opponents' eyes- what remained was murderous rage. With a bellow, the older man launched a ferocious assault, wielding both rapier and dagger like a windmill. A classically-trained fencer would have found this no problem but Tom did not have that sophistication in his background and he panicked. He blocked some of the blows but the weight and sheer ferocity of the attack pushed him backwards until he fell back on a patch of grass and his dagger was knocked from his hand.

Pembroke approached slowly. "Isn't the gentlemanly thing to allow your opponent to retrieve his weapon?" asked Tom hopefully.

Tom looked around him. None of the other young men would step in to help. Edmund, who might have tried, was being held back by Pembroke's men. Pembroke was the dominant force and he knew it. Tom was done for. Pembroke stood over him, raised his arm but then somehow it stayed magically in mid-air.

Tom scrambled to his feet. The sword arm of his opponent was held firmly in place by the fencing master who had returned unnoticed and slipped through the group to arrest the fight just in the nick of time.

"I can see I'm going to have to keep an eye on you," he said, staring at Pembroke, with whom he'd had similar problems before. "Both of you." He turned to Tom whom he didn't recognise but these spoiled rich boys looked much the same these days, even if the boy's clothes seemed more like that of a common labourer.

The moment passed and Tom regained his composure. He even got some pats on the back. Pembroke held his gaze slightly longer than felt comfortable and promised that he would see him again. Tom gave a weak smile, breathing a sigh of relief.

Taking the earliest opportunity, Tom begged his leave and grabbing Edmund, the pair staggered off to where Ned had been following events from a distance. Crouching down behind the hedge once more, the recriminations began.

"You crazy idiot," spat Tom. "You could have got us both killed."

"Me? You were the one trying to best Pembroke there." Edmund softened his tone as he realised what he'd done. "You won't tell Will, will you?"

"He may not have to," interrupted Ned. He held up Edward's ripped jacket. Tom and Edmund exchanged anxious glances. "Now we really will be for it."

Chapter Eight
All the World's a Stage

'All the world's a stage
And all the men and women merely players.'
(*As You Like It*, II, (vii), l. 138-139)

The fact that Tybalt had few scenes and one of them involved a fight with Mercutio, meant that Tom spent quite a while rehearsing with Edmund who he soon realised was like a child with little ability to concentrate. Happily, his rehearsal was interrupted. Less happily, it was due to Will's question about a damaged costume.

Will inspected their best gallant's costume and frowned at what appeared to be grass stains on one elbow, a few rips and even some apparent blood stains on one side.

"Ned, Tom," he called. "Come here." With a grimace, they obeyed. "What's the meaning of this?" He held up the evidence.

"Ah," said Ned, reddening. "Er, I er…"

"It looks like someone's been duelling in this. It won't do, I tell you. Well?"

"Er, I, well-"

"-Because I don't need to tell you how much we have invested in this company, including my one eighth share. Do you know what I think?"

"Er, I can't imagine…sir," replied Ned nervously. But he could really. He shut his eyes and waited for the full wrath of his master.

"I think…you and Tom here. I think that between you…you've tried to age this costume on purpose. Tried to give it the appearance of having been in combat." Ned opened both eyes, disorientated like one who has been long-blindfolded and then exposed to the light. "Deliberately given it a few marks as if it has already been used. Very accurately too, if I may say so. And-" he held up his hand as Ned tried to speak. "-It's very sweet of you, really it is but I must insist that we do no further damage to the merchandise. "Is that clear?"

"Perfectly," replied Ned, breathing out slowly.

Will came and watched Tom rehearsing, or trying to, with Edmund. "Any problems, Tom?"

He could hardly say what the real difficulty was but he had other questions. "How do I know when a scene has ended?"

It sounded stupid but Will did not take it as such. "Often I'll close a scene with a rhyming couplet." Tom looked at him blankly. "You know, two lines that rhyme. But in general, you see players coming and going on stage, so their opening lines are particularly important and usually they speak as they move, not waiting to be centre-stage."

"And how shall I depart the stage?"

"Well, do not rise from the dead. As Mercutio, you are but a corpse, remember. Your lifeless body could be carried from the stage by your kinsmen- Romeo and a few others. A better choice would be to manage to die off-stage."

"I could help," offered Edmund.

"You too lie dead, Master Tybalt. We need a similar solution for your corpse." He had hoped that Mercutio's death- accidentally hit under Romeo's arm as he sought to separate Tybalt from Romeo, might serve as a lesson for Edmund but that seemed a little hopeful. "Under no circumstances are you to get up and start dancing about on stage. Do you understand?"

"Yes," replied Edmund with little enthusiasm. His hopes for his first dramatic role had been a little unrealistic. He had expected to at least play the handsome hero. Then he brightened a little. "You told me not to get carried away." He started to laugh at his own joke.

"Yes, little brother," replied Will drily. "Very amusing. Oh, by the way Tom, since you read so well, there is another role which may suit you." Tom just looked at him blankly. Again. "Usually, as I said, the opening lines or actions of a scene define its time and place. In *Romeo and Juliet*, when Romeo and his friends go to the Capulet party, they march about the stage- that represents the journey. We do not need to see it all. Occasionally though, we use a Greek-style Chorus, a figure who comes on stage and tells the audience what has happened or what will happen. There is one at the beginning of *Romeo and Juliet* and he appears once more later on. I'd like you to be the Chorus."

There was a pause. "But how can I play two parts? Mercutio appears shortly after the second Chorus."

"Well remembered, young Tom. In that case we could cut the second Chorus speech. Tis a shame for you perhaps with fewer lines but truth to tell, it adds little."

"Are we allowed to do that?" asked Tom, a little nervously. It was the second time that he had asked that question in recent days.

"Allowed?" Will let out a full-throated laugh. "It is my play. I wrote it. If I want to cut something out, then I will do it. Adding material is perhaps more difficult. We must have a licence to perform from The Master of the Revels but to remove lines? That is our choice. And more to the point, who will ever know? The audience cannot check with some sort of…book, can they?" Not for the first time, Tom thought that the idea of an audience reading the plays seemed ridiculous.

"It is very important to be loud enough and clear in your speech. You have some lungs, young Tom, yes? The yard can get very noisy and not everyone will be hanging on every word. They cannot look back and re-read something like in a book. So there is an element of repetition of important points and audiences generally accept this."

Tom had a further question about his role as Chorus. "Won't the audience know what happens?"

"Yes," replied Will simply. There was a further pause, during which Will realised Tom expected more. "Oh, I see. Well, the most important thing is how the story happens. It's like a joke- it is in the manner of the telling that brings the most pleasure. The story itself is not new. Arthur Brooke wrote a poem of this very tale but I have added elements of my own. I have added you Tom- there is no Mercutio and no Chorus in the Brooke version." Tom felt strangely proud to be bringing something new.

"Two great families, the Montagues and the Capulets have a long-running feud in the Italian town of Verona. This conflict breaks out anew and it is only by the actions of two lovers, Romeo from the Montagues and Juliet, from the Capulets that the feud is ended although it costs their lives."

He quickly checked through the lines that Will placed into his hands. He'd heard them of course as prompter but it was only now lines that Tom became aware of something else. The opening Chorus speech was short- 14 lines but it also rhymed in a specific pattern. He whistled softly to himself. It was a sonnet. Another of Will's little games, sometimes with himself, sometimes with his audience.

Will had begun to move away but stopped as if remembering something. "And don't worry. Ned will teach you how to breathe."

"I beg your pardon?" answered Tom. "I thought you just said that Ned can teach me to breathe." He chuckled, assuming this was a joke.

"Look," said Ned later as he and Tom stood in the middle of the stage. "The only way to deliver your lines is if you project your voice, from here." He gestured to his stomach. "If you don't, the crowd won't hear you. It's not like we have some kind of magic way to make our voices louder, except controlling your breathing. I expect your throat is sore?"

Tom cleared his throat. "It's a little…scratchy," he admitted begrudgingly.

"Well, we'll practice with breathing."

"I think I know how to breathe."

"Well, it's up to you. But you have rehearsal and performance every day here. Without training, you'll lose your voice completely in a day, two at most. Then you cannot stay here. We need people who can work but also people who can listen and learn. Can you listen and learn, Tom Swann?"

Tom's performance, the following days met with some audience enthusiasm. His recital of the Chorus seemed to be a success. He remembered to breathe as Ned had shown him and although he ended the speech a little breathless, in the coming days, he came to appreciate the advice. In his dramatic exit as Mercutio, Tom even managed to gain a bitter laugh from the crowd with his dying words, "Ask for me tomorrow and you shall find me a grave man."

Usually, they ate their main meal at midday, but on the first day of *Romeo and Juliet*, they gathered in the early evening to discuss progress and future plans at the Tabard Inn, the nearest tavern to The Globe. Or as several of the company thought of it, a chance to eat and drink until their guts exploded. The Landlord, known only as Harry, produced a wide selection of foodstuffs, which to Tom's eyes seemed little short of a feast fit for a King. As usual, everything was covered with a sticky sugar glaze (except Harry), including the poultry, possibly to hide how old the meat was.

"Potato?" Harry was very proud of the very latest in culinary sophistication and came to offer his regular customers this very special delicacy. As he spoke, Tom noticed not only that he had gaps in his teeth but that he had deliberately blackened others to give them the appearance of corruption. It was important to give the impression that you were getting plenty of sugar.

The question hung in the air but Heminges pulled a face. This new vegetable had become fashionable with well-to-do customers but many people regarded it with suspicion, some even wondering if it was poisonous on account of a certain similarity in appearance with deadly nightshade. Several new products had been brought back from the New World but Tom wasn't sure about them. Rich men (and sometimes women) would smoke tobacco, which seemed very strange to him and apparently you could chew that too.

They ate well. Before he had joined the company, he had mostly survived on stale, black rye bread and porridge. There was always a small amount of milk, eggs and vegetables as such items were thought of as peasant food but now he ate meat much more regularly, even fish on Friday, and not the kind of meat he was used to, like chicken. The players ate game, like duck, pheasant and partridge as well as delicacies, like blackbird and lark. Tom had forgotten how hungry he used to be, often going days without proper food. Since he'd been working at The Globe, he had filled out and grown, physically as well as in emotional terms. Will made sure they were all well-fed. He knew how hard the job was and not having enough to eat would not make it easier.

After eating until he felt his stomach would burst, Tom went, slowly, back to The Globe to pick up some pages of script that he had forgotten and needed to read for the following day. Dusk was fast approaching and the light from the low sun would soon be gone.

He lay on his back, gazing up at heaven. Not the real one- he was lying in the middle of the stage, looking up the elaborately-painted underside of the roof. There was the sun, the moon and all the signs of the zodiac as well as Apollo and Mercury, hopefully to inspire eloquent speech and the muses of comedy and tragedy. Even Fame was blowing her trumpet but Tom couldn't imagine it would blow for him. A cloud helped conceal a central trap that led up to the hut. The images were separated into panels by golden borders or so-called frets. Ned had told him that the gold was not just paint but actual gold. He wasn't sure if he believed that but it certainly gave off a golden glow.

The colours were no less impressive than the artwork. Blues, gold and even some vibrant red in places all vied for attention- it was like nothing he had ever seen. He had, like most people his age and class, grown up knowing nothing of art and painting and while he knew it existed in theory, this was the first time he had ever seen art of such vibrant quality. He lay back and breathed deeply, trying to comprehend the skill of creating such a wonder.

Will came and joined him. Neither of them spoke for a while. "All our world is here," he said eventually. "Up there, the heavens. Down there-" he pointed to the trap in the stage floor- "is hell. And we, we are caught for but a brief time, here in the middle."

Another pause fell upon them. "Do you think people will remember you?" asked Tom suddenly. "In the future, I mean."

Will was used to Tom's questions by now, which sometimes appeared to come out of nowhere and he thought for a moment. "Perhaps. But I am not the important thing here. It is the work. Always the work. I just write plays."

Tom sat up. "These are not just plays, Will. And yes, I know you write poems too. I mean, there is all of life here in these pages. I know

I have not read them all but there are stories of love and hate and passion. Of mistaken identities, confusion in love, tragic ambition and death. And all of this in words I'm sure no-one has ever heard before."

"That's only because I make some up."

"But that too, is wonderful."

"Do you think so?"

"I do. I really do."

Tom lay back again and looked up at the stars. "Do you think our destiny is mapped out there?"

"Those who charge to tell fortunes would have us believe so."

Tom turned and looked at Will. There were times when he wondered whether he wasn't some kind of sorcerer able to cast spells over those around him.

When Tom left in the evening, Will was often still scribbling by a fading candlelight and on entering in in the morning, thinking he was the first, he would find Will asleep in much the same spot, suggesting he had just snatched a few hours' sleep in a chair. When Will was feeling inspired, 'when the muse was with him' as he called it, it almost felt to Tom like being in the presence of a firework. Spectacular, apparently uncontrollable but also destined to burn itself out far too soon.

Chapter Nine

Ned has a Special Present for Tom

'The apparel oft proclaims the man.'
(*Hamlet*, I, (iii, l. 72)

Edmund had been sleeping at Tom's house. Edmund thought it was because he was now an important player and needed a bodyguard but really Will wanted someone to keep an eye on his wayward brother. As far as Tom's mother was concerned, Edmund was just another beggar, which ironically was a more accurate description of him.

As usual, getting Edmund to the playhouse on time was far from easy. "Come ON, screamed Tom. "Or we'll be late." He had to virtually drag Edmund from his bed and push him every inch of the way like a shepherd with a reluctant sheep.

As they approached a particularly narrow street with overhanging windows, as if by instinct, Tom suddenly stopped but Edmund kept walking. Tom pointed a warning but that only made Edmund look up. "Why have you-?" At that moment, he was drenched from a shower of some kind of liquid from above. He wished he had kept his mouth shut too.

"City life is not all excitement," Tom said seconds later, patting a rather green-faced Edmund gently on the back while he vomited heartily into a ditch. "Some of it's excrement." Perhaps Edmund needed less a guard-of-honour and more a wet-nurse.

Tom and Edmund entered the playhouse, only just on time and were making themselves busy, when Burbage strode in, clutching a few hurriedly-written sides. He did not look entirely happy. "Will, Will."

"Yes," Will looked up from his table. Tom had been there long enough to know that he did not always take kindly to interruptions but Burbage was their most important player and a fellow sharer. What he got away with others could not. "What kind of play is this?" He held up his papers as if that made everything clear.

Will did not immediately reply. In fact, he took so long, Burbage was on the verge of repeating his question, thinking that he had not been heard. "It's a…mixture. There is a love story, there is poetry, there are songs. It is a pastoral."

"And you think city folk will like it?"

Will shrugged. He knew how difficult it was to try and predict the reaction of the public. "Who knows?"

"But is there a marriage?" A note of exasperation was creeping into Burbage's voice. "Does it end well?"

Will smiled. But it somehow had sadness in it too. "Some might say marriage is the end of happiness, not its beginning. Yes." Burbage visibly relaxed. He needed people to go away satisfied and wanting to come back with their pennies the following week or even the following day if they could afford it. "Four."

"Four?"

"At the moment, there are four marriages."

"Is that good?"

"You must decide that for yourself. What you will. And there are songs," added Will.

"Songs?"

"Yes."

"In a pastoral?"

"Yes. Don't look at me like that. There are plenty of lovers separated, some philosophy, a wrestling match. And songs."

Burbage squinted at him. "It's not another *Measure for Measure* is it?" That had not been well received.

"If I just write what the crowds want, they could all do that for themselves."

"Now Will, you know that's wishful thinking. Most of them cannot hold a quill, let alone write."

"But they have thoughts and feelings. They have souls. I want my plays to be more than just…entertainment."

"Yes, Will, you might want that but entertainment is the name of the game. I need a play for this week and one for the next. One that will fill the house, not empty it. That is my dream. The world is full of starving artists."

"I would rather have the soul of an artist than the heart of a rich man."

"Well, I think we'll have to agree to disagree on that."

As prompter, Tom read the plays more thoroughly than anyone. He soon realised that he was at the centre of something quite extraordinary. The plays were…how could he describe them? Great stories, certainly. The crowds flocked to The Globe day after day. But there was more. Due to his familiarity with the words, Tom felt that at some level, although he had only been with the company a short time, he knew Will in a way that others did not. How could Will find these words- the law, hunting, history, philosophy, even the processes of tanning leather- a multitude of subjects seemed to fall naturally within his scope. And yet Ned had said that he left school at 15. What kind of man can know so much and express it so well?

Such musings were passing through his head while sweeping one of the upper galleries. As if summoned by his own power of thought, he heard a creak behind him and whirled around to see Will sitting right up at the back in the shadows, almost unseen but from where he could observe all the business of the playhouse laid out before him. He had brought paper, quill and a pot of ink with him, which at least explained the blotchy mess in one of the back seats that he had been on the verge of complaining about to Cuthbert.

"Will?"

"Ye-e-e-es," answered Will, not looking up from his nib as it scratched its way across the paper.

"I was just wondering. From where do your ideas arise?"

The scratching stopped. "Ah," he replied with a sigh and looked up at Tom's eager face. He was used to people asking such things. He did not answer straight away but sat back and looked out straight in front of him. "I can write of murder but am I an assassin? No." Tom had never heard that word before but he could guess its meaning. "My plays are of lords and Kings but am I high-born? No. I can speak of fairies and witches, but have I ever seen one? No." He stood up stiffly and came down towards Tom. "I'll tell you where my ideas come from." He beckoned Tom closer until they were but an arm's length apart. Will put a forefinger to his head. "From here."

Tom frowned. He was only a 13-year-old beggar boy and Will Shakespeare was…well, Will Shakespeare. And he had shown him nothing but kindness. And yet…"I have some…questions too about the new play."

As You Like It was a fearsomely-complicated piece of work, involving groups of characters separated, undergoing trials and then finally meeting up again and falling in love. Will had talked of Tom being right for the part of Rosalind but upon looking at the 'sides' (that's what the players called the text describing their part), Tom seemed far from sure. He decided to tackle Will about it.

"It's about Rosalind."

"What about her?"

"Well, look how many lines she has."

"I know, Tom. I wrote them, remember."

"Yes of course, sorry." He had been encouraged since his first day at the playhouse to question everything, including Will, when really he had no right to do so.

"I have been quite careful," Will continued. "I have made Rosalind 'more than common tall' and as elsewhere, like Viola in *Twelfth Night* and Portia in *The Merchant of Venice*, I have her dressing up as a boy in some places just to make it easier. It's perfect for you."

"What do you mean? She speaks almost half the lines of the play."

"Exactly. You are a talented actor, boy. This is your chance to show the world what you can really do. And as I've written this, it means you can play both a man and a woman."

"What?"

"Think- Rosalind pretends to be Ganymede and then in the Forest of Arden, she, well he really, offers to help the hero, Orlando by pretending to be a girl for him to express his love."

Tom spoke his thoughts aloud, trying to make sense of this. "So you have a boy, me,…playing a girl… playing a boy…playing a girl?"

"Put simply, yes."

"My head hurts."

"Go and see Ned."

"Why? Does he have a cure for headaches?"

Will smiled. "He has something else for you."

As Tom entered the tiring-house, Ned was busy as usual, his shrunken left hand deftly and speedily adding a row of buttons to a luxurious velvet dress. Such was Ned's energy and enthusiasm that Tom hadn't really appreciated how his weaker arm did not seem to stop him from sewing and creating the most intricate garments. Neither this, nor his misshapen leg seemed to slow him down but he confided to Tom that it had stopped him from playing heroines. He was a player too but was consigned to minor roles like servants.

It was just a cruel fact of life that as Tom walked the streets as a beggar, he was surrounded by physical deformity that the powers of medicine could not cure.

Ned looked up. "Perhaps now is the time to introduce you to Lucius."

Tom looked round but apart from themselves, the small room was empty.

Ned brought up his other hand that had been below the table out of sight. It contained a medium-sized rat. "It gets a bit lonely back here in the tiring-house. I found him one day up in one of the galleries. Quite an aristocratic rat. He's a good mouser."

They did suffer at The Globe from mice at times, being near the river, having lots of food dropped out in the yard and not being so far from the city that really was teeming with rodent life. Tom had heard of cats that chased mice but rats? Still, he thought as he watched Lucius' pink nose inspect Will's prose for signs of interest, he was quite sweet.

Lucius then moved across the room and began snuffling around in a far corner by a chest of elaborate royal costumes as if he was wondering whether they would fit him.

Will came in, mainly to pick up some papers that lay scattered over his writing table. He paused when he spotted the unwelcome visitor. "Do you have to bring that thing in here, Ned?"

"It's harmless."

"That remains to be seen. It ate my bread and cheese yesterday."

"Well, don't leave food lying around."

"So, it's my fault is it?"

"He's just doing what comes naturally."

"Well, so am I. If I catch it, Ned, it will be the flattest rat in Christendom." He marched out with the sides that he had been looking for.

"No," shouted Ned and pretended to cover Lucius' ears, who didn't look especially worried by the threats being made to his life. He looked up at Tom. "He doesn't do any harm and he keeps me company." He turned back to his next piece of work- an elaborate courtier's jacket. Ned was the best tailor in the company. Any holes, patches, buttons or complete reworking that was necessary- he was the one to save the day.

Tom found himself staring at Ned's shrunken arm. "How can you?..."

"I know, yellow and red together. It looks terrible."

"No, I mean…" He hesitated a second time.

"I know." Twas but a jest. Now, first things first. Still concentrating on the jacket, he handed Tom a white garment with his right hand.

"What's this?"

"A petticoat."

"A petticoat?" repeated Tom.

Ned nodded. "A lot of the costumes are quite stiff to the touch. If you don't wear something like that, after a very short while, you'll be sore and itching all over. You don't want that."

"I don't want that," agreed Tom.

"Go on then. Put it on."

"Over my other clothes?"

"Well, this is just a trial but take your other things off."

"Everything?" Tom was not prudish and on the street, he had seen all kind of nakedness but he felt a little shy here.

Ned rolled his eyes. "Just down to underclothes will do for today." Tom reddened in embarrassment but obeyed. "My," Ned added, observing the grubby, grey specimens that Tom was wearing. "We'll have to get you some new things or you'll spoil the stock."

"Right, what now?"

"This." Ned handed him something much smaller. "It's a bodice. Here, let me." Ned stood behind him, wrapped the bodice round Tom's upper body and then pulled the laces at the back tight, making Tom gasp.

"Careful," he nearly choked.

"Sorry but we've got to create a waistline for you. Like an hour-glass, see." He proceeded to pull the series of laces even tighter, finishing off with a double-bow. "There. How do you feel?"

"Like a parcel," croaked Tom.

"Now," said Ned, producing a strange contraption and setting it in front of Tom. "Just step into that, would you?"

It was a round, white frame with hoops inside it to give the whole thing shape. Ned could see Tom's puzzled expression. "It's called a farthingale. It will give you the shape we need."

"Will it?" said Tom, still struggling to breathe. He thought it would make him look like a giant cake. Nevertheless he did what he was told.

"This one's got whalebone hoops, so it's a bit heavier than the ones that use wire," explained Ned. "Now all we need is a roll," he added, wrapping a bulky belt around Tom's waist, giving him more of a typically female shape. "Then there's a skirt," said Ned, starting to put another garment over Tom's head. It was covered in elaborate embroidery, which was probably quite artfully done but Tom found most of his concentration had to be devoted to breathing and not going blue and dying.

"Now, all that's left-"

"-There's more?" croaked Tom in a slightly higher voice.

"Of course. Dear me, you do like to complain, don't you? Imagine if you were an actual woman. You'd have to do this every day." Tom had never had such admiration for the female sex before. "Now, all that's left is the actual dress." He lifted an elaborate blend of satin and silk over Tom's head. "There."

"Are we done?" wailed Tom.

"Nearly," lied Ned. "All we need to do now is sort out a wig and some make-up to give you the proper pale complexion of a noblewoman. I like to use a mix of talc, tin and my own special ingredient," he added, dropping his voice to a whisper, "lead. Then, add a bit of cinnabar to give you some rosy cheeks and you're all ready to begin to learn how to walk, sit and talk like a lady. We'll go easy as it's your first rehearsal but you'll need to spend a few hours a day practising, if you want the crowds to accept you as a woman and not throw things at you. Now, I'm sure you know the laws surrounding clothing?"

Sumptuary laws dictated what could and could not be worm by different classes. There were strict codes of behaviour about who might wear what kinds of clothes and even colours. Tom had grown up with such ideas and considered them entirely normal. Only barons could wear silver cloth and the idea of peasants wearing silk was just absurd. Everyone knew their place and stayed in it. He nodded.

"Well, here players may wear what they want. Not when rehearsing but on stage. It is like a…" He searched for the word. "A dream where you can be whoever you want to be."

Tom thought for a moment. He began to see now why quite so many people flocked to The Globe every day.

Several days later, Ned was bustling around, talking while holding several pins in his mouth, which just made Tom nervous. The performance was due that afternoon and he was still cutting cloth and making adjustments. Changes in casting, sometimes forced upon them by illness of players, had major consequences for Ned and his team of skilled tailors. Teams of women would add embroidered designs to items like gloves and apprentice boys would scurry back and forth through the city's dark, narrow and often extremely muddy streets to fetch and carry garments requiring adjustment. Woe betide them if any of the mud was spattered on the costumes.

Tom was standing and Ned was altering his cuffs. The model was clearly not happy.

"Will you keep still?"

"How long will this take?"

"As long as necessary. Now, try not to move or I might leave a pin in by mistake. Ned had admitted he did that on purpose sometimes for members of the cast who thought they were above the rest. Jake's name was mentioned.

Will strode in and cast a knowledgeable eye over the costume rail. "And mind that velvet cloak, Ned. Make sure you keep it of the sun." Will was especially aware of the expense involved in the elaborate dyes and fabrics. Upon their death, players sometimes left their costumes as amongst their most valuable possessions.

Tom gave another heavy sigh and Ned rolled his eyes at Will.

"Come now, master Swann," said Will. "We must look our best."

"Why?"

"Why?" There was a note of exasperation in his voice. "Do you not see how finely-balanced our fortunes are? Yes, on a good-day we can live like Kings. Good weather, a full house, a popular play and all is fine. The next week? Rain, only a few seats taken- the result? We have nothing to feed our children."

Tom was about to point out that he had no children but thought better of it. Will continued,

"Now, if we can impress an empty-headed Lord, perhaps with a verse or two about the beauty of his wife, his family home, goodness perhaps even his own physical beauty, then we will do this. It puts bread in our mouths, Tom. Now do you see?"

Tom nodded. Will watched him. He was a quick learner but he still was quite naïve for his age. He'd have to toughen up if he wanted to survive this lifestyle.

"It's a hard business. We must keep the place full by writing and performing plays that people want to see. Because if we don't, there are other places that will."

By 'other places' Tom realised he meant places like The Theatre and The Curtain. They were all finding life hard but others added to their revenue with animal baiting shows of various kinds, typically bears but also dogs, cows, even horses sometimes. It so happened the design of The Globe made this difficult but Tom was glad- he never enjoyed the spectacle of animals ripping each other to shreds.

"Even Jonson, the great Ben Jonson, with the benefit of a university education and a noble patron was still imprisoned for his play *The Isle of Dogs*. We all lead a charm'd life." Will's attention returned to the costume rail. "Ah, yes, Ned. We shall need some pearl-encrusted leather gloves for the County Paris." From his work as a prompt, Tom knew that Paris was Romeo's love rival in *Romeo and Juliet* and born of a rich family.

"Right," said Ned. "When for? Next month?" Will pulled a face. "Next week? Oh, come on, Will, I cannot perform the impossible. You are joking? Tomorrow?"

"I'm only asking because you are such a great worker of miracles. Do your best." He gave Ned a pat on the shoulder and vanished as soon as he had entered.

Ned shook his head. "I don't understand how he gets away with it." He gave a rueful smile. "I just know that he does."

Ned was open and friendly, answering all of Tom's many questions with patience. The two soon grew to be close friends and Tom loved to watch both the performance but also Ned's unseen organisation, like a puppeteer controlling the show.

"Oh, look at that."

Tom peeked through the drape alongside Ned. "What?"

Ned pointed at a man taking his seat on the uppermost gallery. He was very ostentatiously-dressed with a huge ruff.

"Who is that?"

"I think he's some kind of earl." Ned shook his head. "Everything was bigger in the 80s." The object of their derision looked like someone who was desperately trying to be fashionable but was receiving rather poor advice.

"Hang on," Tom almost cried out in surprise "It's Pembroke!"

"Shh, keep your voice down."

"It is! It's him," managed Tom between giggles. "Look."

Ned took a closer look. "Oh, my." He had so many different colours and fabrics, the overall effect was like an explosion in a tailor's workshop. His shoes had slightly higher heels than normal, giving him more height but making him totter when he moved, making it hard for him to find his seat, almost stumbling into other nobles who clearly were unimpressed. His hat was topped off with a huge ostrich feather. Finally, he lurched into a seat, took off the said object but then continued to hold the hat in front of him, almost as if he was desperate for them to notice how expensive it was.

Audiences expected to see opulence and spectacle, especially in the matter of costume. Some companies fell into debt to pay for their costumes but Will was reluctant to do this. Or if he did, they never knew of it. This was possible as he would disappear off to Stratford for days at a time sometimes, returning often with a darker countenance than when he left. The Globe was producing good money but all of them were working so hard, they had no time or energy to spend much of it.

Anyway, it was a constant battle to keep costs under control. Keeping check on stock was obviously important and hefty fines were charged on any player who left the playhouse still in costume. Wherever possible, these important assets were kept under lock and key in chests in the tiring-house or up in the hut, to keep them safe both from thieves and the attention of moths. There was a constant struggle to make offers for elaborate items and due to the speed of changing fashions at court, there was a steady black market in clothing sold off to servants who would then bring them to The Globe for sale. The death of a nobleman often led to a flurry of offers to buy his clothing like rats feasting on a corpse. At first, Tom found this unseemly but after a few short weeks, he was fully involved in the deal-making process himself and proved very adept at running a hard bargain.

"Right, so what have we got?" asked Will about that week's haul. The company were gathered on stage like pirates dividing up stolen treasure. Tom held up one rather sorry-looking jacket.

"Have you checked for valuables?"

"I've looked in the pockets," said Tom gloomily. "There's nothing."

"Really, Tom. I wonder about you sometimes." He took the garment from him. "I don't mean just all the obvious places." He reached into the lining of one of the sleeves and deftly producing a razor-sharp knife from his belt (at which Tom recoiled slightly) flicked at the cuff and gave it a shake. There was a double-thud as two small objects fell to the ground.

Tom pounced upon them like a hungry cat. Shaking and blowing off the dirt, he raised his hand to Ned and opened his palm. There were two small but clearly gold rings, each engraved and bearing a hallmark indicating significant worth.

"See, Tom. The truly interesting things are not for all eyes to see. They are in the dark places.

Some trades take years to learn. The stage is no exception but the best way to learn is to do. Many occupations have guilds that mean a boy your age would not be anything more than an apprentice for years. Here, the apprentices are the life-blood of our business. As soon as you can do a job, you do it- behind the stage, as a player, as…whatever. Stick close to Ned. He will guide you in what you need to learn."

And so it was. Over the following days, Tom practised many hours a day and soon mastered the basics of dress, voice and deportment that were necessary if he was to be a credible heroine. The clothes that Ned made were designed for rapid changes, not for wearing on the street and Tom soon came to appreciate the ingenuity and artistry of his new friend. It still took him a long time to prepare but never as long as that first time. He practised, made mistakes, learned and got better.

Ned was also endlessly patient in helping with Tom's poor stage-fighting technique and even taught him some French and Italian via all the terms used to describe different movements._Soon he was proficient with most forms of blade, the rapier in particular. Will said that most gentlemen were trained to use a sword and might boo them off if fight scenes were poorly performed.

He watched Burbage and Condell rehearsing their fights with an increasing sense of admiration and rushed forward to help when Burbage was badly wounded. He was amazed to be met by the two men both throwing their heads back and laughing. It was only then that they showed him the pig's bladder filled with blood that Burbage had hidden in his doublet. It became apparent that they had planned this trick for days and Tom was the source of much merriment in the company but he didn't mind.

He had to rehearse his own lines, along with helping others learn theirs. It was an incredibly intense lifestyle and yet Tom loved every minute. It was not being the focus of attention that drew him, although he could see that for others like Armin, they were like flowers that bloomed in the sunshine. It was partly the nervous excitement of things going wrong, lines being forgotten and props failing to work but more than this, it was the chance to tell stories. And what stories they were. The tales that dripped from Will's pen were the stuff of dreams. He had been told that his father had taken him to the playhouse when he was much younger but if he was honest, of the actual plays themselves, he remembered little. Now, he could see, in minute detail, the wonderful slapstick humour in *A Comedy of Errors*, the murderous ambition in *Julius Caesar* and the moving love-story of *Romeo and Juliet*.

Tom tried to rehearse with Edmund and Ned on the stage under Will's watchful gaze. Will had given Rosalind plenty of lines that was true and there were some good ones in there, like the fun she makes of men who have 'a swashing and a martial outside' but are really cowards underneath. Was he thinking of Edmund here? Rosalind's best friend, Celia, who joins her in running away to Arden, was played by Ned, so they had plenty of fun in rehearsal, especially when Ned described Orlando (played by Gough) as pining for love and how they 'found him under a tree liked a dropped acorn.'

Edmund found concentration difficult and began describing the beauty of the woman from the carriage they had glimpsed at Shoreditch and how he could not survive another day if he never saw her again.

"Oh, come now, Edmund. No man, ever died for love." At this, he was provoked into a show of outrage and ranted at Tom for several minutes before he could be calmed. "No, Edmund it is a line of Rosalind's in the play."

"Oh, I see."

"But it is also true."

Tom looked around him but the stage was virtually bare, except for a simple, wooden bench. "How do we…?" His question tailed off. "I mean, how do the audience know where we are?"

"That's what the words are for," answered Ned, a little sarcastically. "When Lorenzo says in *The Merchant of Venice*, 'The moon shines bright, in such a night as this,' we know what time of day it is. If no-one comments upon it, you may trust it is of little importance."

"And what do I do?" gasped Edmund jumping up and down like a small child.

"You play Charles," explained Ned.

"And what is he?"

"Charles…is the Duke's champion wrestler." Condell stood by, wondering how he was going to teach Edmund how to stage-fight without killing his opponent. Or himself.

"Really?" Edmund's chest puffed out a little.

"You've earned it, little brother," chipped in Will.

"But, I cannot read well." He blushed with embarrassment.

"Tis no matter. Charles is a man of action. Very like yourself. A man of few words. None in fact."

"So I do not have to learn any lines?"

"None whatsoever." In truth, Edmund had struggled with the spoken element of Tybalt's part. "Just wrestle like a demon."

"That I shall. And thank you, kind brother." He threw his arms around Will who could do little but stand there until he was released again.

"Now, you will have to train so that you look like a professional wrestler. Put a bit of muscle on those bones. And you'll be working with Condell here. He is the company's expert on such matters, so make sure you listen well to his instruction." Will muttered under his breath to Condell. "He gets beaten by Orlando, the hero but break it to him gently, alright?"

When it came to performance, there was so much to do, time passed like a blur. Tom had so much to worry about with his costume, his lines and trying to make sure no-one else forgot theirs that before he was aware of it, it was time for the 'All the world's a stage' speech by Jacques (played by Will). The company had got snatches of this in rehearsal but the whole speech sent shivers up the spines of all those who heard it. He described the seven ages of life, from the mewling and puking babe to the whining schoolboy with his shining morning face,' which Tom recognised from Will's description of his own schooldays.

Then came 'the lover' sighing with the heat of a furnace which made him think of Gough and all the hearts he would break. Next was 'the soldier,' seeking honour and quick in quarrel- this was Edmund of course. Then came 'the justice,' fat and happy to judge others. The figure of the preaching Puritan outside The Globe strangely came to mind. Then, there was the older man, shrunken in size and having little left of his youthful strength. Here he thought of his own sick mother but possibly of his father too and what he would look like if he were alive today.

And then the final stage, ghastly and slightly horrifying- without teeth, memory and the ability to do anything for himself, a kind of second childishness. He didn't know anyone like that but could see his mother becoming weaker day by day and the tears welled up in his eyes. It was like a wheel that had come full circle. It was natural and the way of things but it still scared Tom sometimes to think about his own mortality.

At the end of the speech, there was absolute silence. It was a moment of reflection but seemed also slightly bitter as if Will was contemplating his own end. At the close of the play, like most comedies, there were marriages certainly, too many to count but as Jacques he took no part in the festivities and seemed an isolated and lonely figure, resolving to go and live in a cave.

For Tom's part, like Rosalind he felt he would 'rather a fool to make me merry than experience to make me sad.' Will had explained that he was seeking to make fun of the current fashion for young men to dress and speak as 'melancholy men,' adopting a mere pose of being sad so people would pay them attention. Still, Tom wasn't sure if Will wasn't taking himself a bit too seriously. The character of Jacques drew a moral from almost everything he saw and judged others for sins he too had committed in the past.

It also fell to Tom to deliver the final words of the play, the epilogue, a duty normally reserved for a man. There were some chuckles amongst the audience when he offered to kiss many of the audience, as 'If I were a woman.' Will knew that Tom would be playing the role and so lines like 'I am not furnished like a beggar' seemed particularly meaningful for one, who until very recently was exactly that and when he made his final curtsey, the crowd in the galleries rose to their feet and the applause was thunderous.

When the crowd had departed, as usual Will brought the company together. They celebrated by sending one of the apprentices out to one of the so-called 'ordinaries,' premises where food could be bought to take away, just round the corner from the playhouse. The boy soon returned with some sheep's feet and black pudding. Tom gagged slightly at the thought of such fayre but after a few tentative bites, he tucked in merrily with the others.

"That was good work today. You all played your parts exceedingly well." His eye came to rest on Edmund who had thrown his wrestler a little harder than necessary and he had needed to step in to stop a real fight from erupting backstage. "Well, mostly. Now then tomorrow we start work on *Macbeth*." Tom gave a sigh. He looked up. "Is something not well, Master Swann?"

Tom struggled to express what he was feeling. "It's just...don't you sometimes wish you could just work on one play, say, for a few weeks rather than producing a different one each day?"

Will chuckled at such a strange notion. "Perhaps but it's what the audience wants that matters. And if we did what you suggest, there's hardly enough people." Tom had the idea that London was endlessly huge. "They are like a child that demands constant and novel entertainment."

"But doesn't that annoy you?"

"Sometimes. But it doesn't change the fact that nearly every day of the week, thousands of people choose to come and see the plays we perform rather than bear-baiting."

Tom wasn't convinced. He thought that quite a few came to the playhouse after visiting the bear-baiting.

After the meal, the older men in the company produced clay pipes, which they proceeded to light.

"Here, boy," said Armin to Tom, offering him one. "Try it. It's good for you." Tom took it but without much enthusiasm. He inhaled a deep breath, held it for a second or two and then exploded in a fit of coughing.

Armin laughed heartily and patted him hard on the back until the coughing subsided. "There, you need to get the hang of it."

Tom had gone pale and handed the pipe back, coughing out some thanks. He would not be buying a pipe. There were a few rich Lords who had taken up the new craze of smoking tobacco but it was very expensive. Tom didn't really think it was sensible to watch your money go up in smoke.

It was dark by the time he reached home. The house was on Goldsmiths' Row in Cheapside, one of a row of near identical alms-houses, designated for the very poorest in society. He and his mother had the right to dwell there due to a favour from a merchant who had served with his father. The man, now dead, had no living relatives and they could not contest the terms of his will as they were so poor. One-by-one, the houses in this street had been bought by a trading company, which had its claws out for theirs too. If they could not pay the rent, they would be thrown out on the street within days.

"It's me, mother," he announced as he came through the door. There were only two rooms in their tiny dwelling but the woman's sight was too poor to identify him and he did not want to alarm her. "I brought you a small chop. Pork."

She had been sitting in her usual spot, staring sightlessly out of the small window next to the door as if viewing a scene of delightful countryside, although there was nothing for Tom to see, except the equally-small house opposite. She roused herself on hearing his voice. "Meat?" She whistled softly. "Not had a good chop for…well, quite a while now. "Begging must have been good today."

He bit his lip. He hadn't told her about the playhouse, about his successes, about his failures about the group of friends he'd found there. She wouldn't understand. For her, the playhouse was a place of sin and she would be ashamed of him. Tears welled up in his eyes. All he'd ever wanted in life was for her to be proud of him. "Yes, begging was good."

Food was still a luxury. It was soon after Tom had been born and he was too young to remember but his mother often spoke of the bad harvest of 94-95 when countless people starved.

"Come, come and talk to your blind mother."

So he did. He sat next to her and told her all about rich gentlemen who stopped by to give a penny to a poor street child and many other untruths, which he embellished with details from his new life at the playhouse.

They had always struggled in life. Too poor for school, he had had to spend his days begging and trying to befriend the dipping gangs that frequented the market. Happiness for him, meant a full belly and no worries about food for the following day. Looking further ahead had never been possible.

Now, he had discovered a whole new life, a new world. Something he was good at and something which he enjoyed. When he put on the costumes and make-up and faced the public trial of performance, he was partly terrified but also partly thrilled.

He had been brought up to see lying as wrong but there was such a thing as a good lie. Tom saw that now. Not a lie to cheat or gain something for yourself but a lie that prevented someone from being hurt. If everyone told the literal truth as the Puritans wanted, there would be no plays, no stories, no poems, except perhaps religious ones. Tom had seen the power of imagination work and he knew that it was magic. Good magic.

After he had cooked the food, tidied away the dishes and cleaned the small room of any dirt that he could see and his mother could not, he lay back on his straw bed and asked his mother to speak on the subject closest to his heart.

"Tell me about father." He liked to hear his mother talk about him, even if it was something he'd heard countless times before. It fed his need to keep a picture in his head.

A dreamy look came onto her face. "Your father was a tall man, big and strong as an oak. We met in Portsmouth where he was about to set sail for the Low Countries. They were carrying a cargo of coal, I think. No, it was wool." She frowned. "No, I was right first time. Definitely coal." His mother would include needless details like this. It used to annoy him and he would be impatient for the real story to start. It was only now that he realised these needless details *were* the story. The rats that nibbled at the ship's biscuits on long voyages, the sight of the stars when his father was far from home, the note of a song that the crew sang to keep their spirits up at an approaching storm. It was the little things that mattered. It wasn't the actual words of his mother that was important, just the soothing tone of her voice that carried him along like floating down a gentle stream.

He fell into a deep sleep and dreamed of himself as one of the nobles who sat at the edge of the stage smoking grand pipes and chipping in advice from time to time to the players who had to accept his words with good grace.

Chapter Ten

Preparing for a Tragedy

'Life's but a walking shadow; a poor player that struts and frets his
hour upon the stage and then is heard no more.'

(*Macbeth*, V, (v), l. 24-26)

Tom liked the comedies- the jokes, the songs, the misunderstandings-
it was all good. But there were times when he felt the hand of the
writer a bit too strongly. Couples would be separated only to be
reunited by the end. Lovers would be married and all would be well.
But he knew, even from his limited experience of life, that all was not
well after marriage.

Furthermore, in *Romeo and Juliet* and *As You like It*, several
couples fell in love at first sight. Tom was suspicious of this. Perhaps
Will was right and in time, he would come to feel the same but how
could you love someone you did not know? Having had to listen to
Edmund, yapping like a small dog about the beauty of any number of
girls whom he only knew from a distance, he was not convinced. He
sounded like Romeo before he ever met Juliet, worshipping a girl
called Rosalyne, a character whom everyone quickly forgot and who
never even appears in the play.

By contrast, when he watched tragedies, the likes of *Hamlet*, he felt
he was taken on a journey. Not by groups of characters who were
separated and then put back together like a child's puzzle but a real
emotional journey with one man from low to high and then low
again. Admittedly the heroes were scarcely low-born to start with but
he cared more about that one man than all the to-ing and fro-ing of

the comedies. He would not dare say this of course to Will, but it was true.

The company had gathered on the stage with a sense of expectation. "What have you got for us, Will?" Armin was already jumping up and down like an over-enthusiastic schoolboy, keen to impress his teacher. There was a genuine sense of excitement amongst the players. Tom had begun to see what a gift some of these parts were for players.

Will held up a hand. "You must be a little patient, my friends. I am trying to find a place for each of your unique talents. Poor, Tom, here for example has never even seen Armin's Bottom."

"Er…." Tom was not sure what to say.

"We've all seen it, haven't we?" The rest of them all nodded solemnly. "Hundreds, nay thousands, flocked to see it. Twas the talk of the town."

There was a further pause as Tom's brain tried to make sense of what he was hearing. "I beg your pardon…?"

"Armin's Bottom," repeated Will, keeping a straight face but only just. "Is a wonder to behold. Famous for it, he is."

"Well, er…" Tom knew that players had a dubious reputation amongst the richer nobility. Maybe it was well-deserved.

It was at this point that Will burst out laughing and the others joined in.

"He's just playing with you Tom," explained Armin. "I played the part of Bottom, the weaver in *A Midsummer Night's Dream*."

"Ah, I see," said Tom with some relief.

"Bottom is a fool who falls in love," explained Will. "He must wear an ass' head in the middle part of the play. Armin is a renowned fool." Tom was puzzled. Working with idiots did not seem a good idea. Will caught his look of incomprehension. "I mean, he is a master at playing the fool.

"Ah, yes," he continued. "Armin can do it all- sing and dance as well as act. And he's even something of a scholar. He has written a book about 'natural fools' like the Fool in *Lear*, compared to so-called 'philosopher fools,' like Touchstone and Feste. He tests what is madness, what is artificial fooling, trying to please others compared to a genuine, real Fool who does not think of himself. He manages somehow to mix what is genuinely mirthful with a darker, sadder spirit.

Tom didn't know about this but he had seen Armin at rehearsal and in performance and his boundless energy was truly a wonder.

"There is a long and honourable tradition here and in other countries too, of a character who is outside time. He speaks nonsense but all-sense. He criticises all but is criticised himself by none. Not even the King. Perhaps especially not the King. Even in plays that do not have a character called a 'fool' some of the same elements appear. There are the most obvious fools like Feste who is an actual jester in *Twelfth Night*, Touchstone in *As You Like It* or the Fool in *King Lear*. But other comic characters have some parts of the fool too, like Bottom in *A Midsummer Night's Dream*, Dogberry in *Much Ado*, even the Nurse in *Romeo and Juliet*, although she's unaware of it- melancholic, wistful but intelligent too. A bit like Hamlet when he is mad or pretends to be. It is a part Armin has made his own.

"Now, in this new play that we must prepare, *Macbeth*, there is no fool as much. It is not a comedy but I want to put a scene in just as Macbeth goes to murder the King. It is partly so we can do some costume business in the tiring-house but time is supposed to pass and I thought now might be the only time to counter the darkness elsewhere in the play. Hence, the Porter." He passed some pages over to Tom. "Now, I want you to run through this with Armin."

"You want me to play in the same scene as Armin?"

"Actually, that won't be necessary. The Porter at the gate is awoken from his slumber by a knocking at the gate. A knocking that gets louder. This scene is just the Porter complaining, there are no other characters in the scene but I have written it in such a way that Will can add some comic business of his own- you'll see. Your job is to help if his memory fails and watch and learn. You think you can do that?" Tom nodded. "And if you ask him nicely, he might show you his Bottom."

The company burst out laughing again.

Macbeth was the tale of an ambitious Scottish lord, Macbeth, who is a loyal supporter of the King, Duncan and shows how that loyalty is turned upside-down when Macbeth meets some witches who appear to tell him his future. He is tempted to kill the King, the worst crime imaginable but has doubts and fears until provoked into action by his scheming wife. That was the part Tom was to play.

The following day, Edmund had managed to get into a small fight with one of the bigger apprentice boys and had been rewarded for his cheek with a punch on the nose. Unfortunately, he had been prancing about in one of the company's best costumes (something Will had told him about on several occasions) and now the front of this was covered in blood.

Tom sat in front of a bucket of water that he had had to bring from the nearest pump outside and was now scrubbing at the garment ferociously, while cursing. "Agh, will these hands never be clean?"

Will, who happened to be passing at that very moment, paused. "Problem, Tom? That looks like blood."

"Er, no. Not at all. A little water clears us of this deed." He carried on scrubbing, trying to get the stain off but with little success. "Will all the soap of the world never get these hands clean?" Will froze as if hearing a voice in his head. "Is everything alright? Are you sick?"

Will shook his head like a puppy at a wasp. "We should be well stocked for soap." He was referring to the soap-works not far off-sometimes the prevailing wind made them wish it was far off. "Anyway, how goes the preparation?"

"Well," said Tom, abandoning Edmund's jacket to soak. "It's this speech where Lady Macbeth calls on the spirits."

"What of it?"

"Well, it's the word that comes next." He hesitated.

"Oh do spit it out, boy. If you cannot say the word to me, how are you going to manage in front of 3,000 people?"

That was a good point. "Un….sex. I mean, I'm not even sure if it is a word."

"Neither am I. What of it?"

"Well, I'm not quite sure, exactly what-"

"-Look, Tom. Lady Macbeth. She is the most ruthless, ambitious woman you can imagine. But at the same time, she loves her husband. The only way she can advance herself at this time is through her husband. And yet, she is a woman of flesh and blood. She has given birth to several children. To embrace evil, she must cast aside all her virtue, all her truth, all her lust for things of the flesh- make herself cold and dead inside. You see?"

"But she is a monster."

Will smiled. "Exactly."

"And there is another word. One of the witches right at the beginning says, where is it, let me see?" He pawed through his sides, which he kept inside his jacket at all times but with hands that were a little wet, making Will wince. "Oh yes. Here, it is. 'Hurly-burly,'" he read slowly. What is that?"

"Oh, you know. When things are all hugger-mugger and skimble-skamble."

"Right."

"Any other questions?"

"Er, well." He ran through a long list of questions about a whole series of words and phrases- 'vanish into thin air,' 'one fell swoop' and 'the milk of human kindness'- but each time, Will answered his questions patiently and with care. "And what is this word? The long one there?"

Will followed Tom's finger that was pointing at the scratchy writing. "'Equivocation.'" Tom just looked at him expectantly. "Oh, I see. Well, it's when someone says something but means another. The witches tell Macbeth that he will be King but they also know this will provoke him into killing the King to speed events along."

"A kind of verbal trickery?"

"Just so. It is the province of lawyers and politicians. They say one thing, knowing someone will take their words to have a different meaning than the one they intend."

"So the purpose is to deceive?"

"Just so. Again. Tis what some of the Gunpowder plotters used to try and escape punishment when asked about their Catholicism." Will paused, lost in thought for a moment. "Language can be razor-sharp but it can also be misleading. The meanings of words can shift and change like fog at sea covering a treacherous reef."

"Oh, and I had another question." He pointed at a word. "What does that say?"

"Can you not read, Tom?"

He felt his face flush red. "Yes, of course. But…the quill is a little hard to see here."

The older man peered over Tom's shoulder. "That is a name. Mine."

"Shaksper," read Tom slowly. He thought it looked like a spider had somehow crawled into a bottle of ink and struggled across the page. But he didn't say this.

"Tell me Tom, have you ever heard anyone in the crowd call out that they didn't like the spelling of a certain word?" Tom shook his head at the strange question. "Exactly. It is a necessary evil but you need lose no sleep over it. Spelling," he said, fixing Tom with both of his pearl-black eyes, "is for dullards."

Tom didn't know quite what he felt about Macbeth. He murdered the King, which was horrible and yet….he was a military hero, he risked everything to get what he wanted and perhaps most admirable of all, he fought on until his last breath, even when he knew his cause was lost. Was he a brave man who overcame his own fears or an evil, ambitious weakling who gave into supernatural temptation? He was all of these things and it was these ideas, some of which contradicted each other, that kept Tom awake sometimes. Not for long though-playhouse life was so hard that usually he collapsed gratefully into his straw bed and slept like a stone until daybreak. Luckily, the dreams that plagued Macbeth did not visit him.

The following day, Will called Tom and Edmund into the tiring-house.

"It is about time for Cuthbert to initiate you two into the dark arts."

"Er, really?" replied Tom nervously.

"Oh, yes. He's quite the wizard, aren't you?" He flashed a smile at Cuthbert who was carefully mixing several mysterious powders together on a nearby table.

"It has been said I can do the impossible." They gazed at him curiously.

"Like making Armin laugh?" suggested Tom. "Like making your brother look bad? Like stopping Edmund fighting?"

Cuthbert looked at the younger Shakespeare's vacant stare. "Perhaps not that impossible. But I can make fire." Edmund's eyes lit up.

"Remember," warned Will sternly. "You are here to learn about stagecraft."

"And why am I there?" piped up Tom.

Will gave a deep sigh as if the answer was obvious. "To keep an eye on Edmund."

"Now," said Cuthbert. "It is important to realise we try and use real fire as little as possible."

"Because of the danger to the building?" asked Tom.

"Partly, yes but it's mainly because it's just hard to control. We could have some smoke out of the trap but we must make sure we don't set the place alight. There are different chemicals to make coloured smoke, like red, yellow, black, and white and with a combination of alcohol and salt we can produce a sudden outburst of flame."

Tom found himself wishing they had used such methods to teach in schools- he would have learned a lot more.

"We use bellows to spread the smoke across the stage but even here you have to be careful. Too much and the crowd cannot see the players and also they may not be able to breathe.

"You don't want the smoke to clear only to reveal a stage littered with dead bodies."

"Er, no, I suppose not," agreed Edmund reluctantly.

"Unless, it's *Hamlet*," noted Tom.

"That's true," agreed Cuthbert.

Edmund looked on alarmed until someone told him later that *Hamlet* ends with a number of fights and deaths.

"Then we can make lightning flashes. Watch." Carefully, he took his mixtures out onto the stage and making sure he was a good distance away from anything and anyone, he selected a small amount of resin from a bag and tossed it into a candle. There was a sudden and violent flash of light. "Be gentle with the gunpowder. The sulphur stinks like rotten eggs and saltpetre is even worse."

"What's that?" asked Tom curiously.

"It's made from dung. Yes, exactly. It stinks and is even worse when it's lit."

Will had reluctantly agreed to let Edmund be one of the witches in the opening scene the following day, so long as he cut down on the cackling. He was allowed to help with the effects too but he nudged a little pile of chemicals into the cauldron for the opening scene, and the entire yard was enveloped in thick smoke, which made everyone cough and their eyes water. By the time it had cleared, not everyone had chosen to stay. Will was furious and had to be held back from striking Edmund.

"You...fool. Do you not realise the precarious state in which we live here?"

"They will come back," said Edmund, unwittingly proving Will's point.

"They'll come back?" spluttered Will in pure rage. "What makes you say that? Do you think they will tell all their friends, 'Oh, do go and see the new play where you can spend an hour coughing and crying before the play has barely begun. You are about as much use as a blunt quill."

Tom was realising that it was not just the life in the playhouse that was changing him but the plays themselves. He felt like he'd jumped into a fast-flowing river but he'd also never felt so alive as he had in the last few weeks. He'd been welcomed- no, it was more than that. He'd been accepted. All those things that made him an outsider on the streets- being tall for his age, some slightly feminine characteristics, an interest in words and performance, above all a sensitivity to the thoughts and feelings of others- all of these things were not weaknesses in the playhouse; they were strengths.

He was having to think about things that he had never considered before and it was like he could feel his brain actually growing inside his head. And playing Lady Macbeth had forced him to consider was she a loyal wife or a temptress to evil? Was she heartless, prepared to smash out the brains of her own baby rather than break a promise or brave in facing her fears, returning to the scene of a grisly murder, which her husband dare not. She was willing to risk damnation to help her husband become King but was she only doing this for her own glory? And did she have a conscience? She said she would have killed the King had he not looked like her father as he slept but was that really true? Maybe she dreamed about her father too. Perhaps she was actually a good person who allowed that goodness to be so overwhelmed by evil that it turned her mad. What little schooling Tom had had was all about learning and repeating, recreating what already existed but this was something else. Here he was thinking, really thinking for himself for the first time in his life and it was an amazing thing to experience.

The other day he had been pondering Lady Macbeth's line, 'The sleeping and the dead are but as pictures.' It wasn't the most important line in the play and yet it set Tom thinking. What really was the difference between sleep and death? When it came to Edmund, not much. He slept like one who was dead and it was almost impossible to rouse him without tipping water over his head (which Will had done some mornings in desperation at the loss of rehearsal time). Perhaps sleep was the way they were being prepared for death? Even the simple line, 'We fail?' uttered during the scene where she manages to persuade Macbeth from absolute resolution not to go through with the murder plan to enthusiastic planning and praise for her courage- these two words could be delivered in any number of ways that sounded accusing, resigned, angry, defiant and many other possibilities. He found himself staring at Will sometimes, marvelling how such thoughts could be passing through the mind of such a man.

Tom tried to raise some of these concerns with Ned. "Do you believe in witches?" Tom tried to sound casual but he had misgivings about witchcraft, especially since he had to perform Lady Macbeth's speech calling on evil powers.

Ned thought long and hard. "I have never seen one but there are many things I cannot explain- the passage of the seasons, changes in the weather, the battle between good and evil in the world. I do know that others believe in creatures that can fly, appear and disappear at will and predict the future." Tom thought of the old woman in the fortune-telling tent. "Some even think they can bring disease, ruin crops, change the weather and sink ships. The King for example."

"James?"

Ned nodded. "Some of it. He has certainly studied the subject He has made witchcraft a capital offence and those charged with witchcraft have been brought to court for examination. Some people believe that witches can control animals like toads, crows and cats and force them to do their bidding."

Tom still wasn't sure. Maybe he just didn't like cats.

"Oh, Ned," Will called across the stage, "I have asked Middleton to write some of the witch scenes."

"Thomas Middleton?" Ned paused in mid-sew. He was sitting on a stool on the stage as the light was better for the threading of needles. Middleton had worked with Will on parts of *Timon of Athens*.

"Yes, I know. Between us, I'm not convinced about some of his material either but he has written well before and I must confess I find writing spells and songs about witches almost impossible. I intend to have witches not just in the background but central to the whole enterprise." He sighed. "James may like it, if nothing else. Perhaps I can write a few lines for Middleton's next play," he added, thinking aloud and headed off to check on supplies of ink and paper.

"Doesn't it worry you?" asked Tom. "Performing works for the King." The playhouse was a great place for rumours and there had been all kinds of talk swirling around the company about James.

Ned gave an unconcerned shrug. "This is nothing new. Not to the older members of the company anyway. It was always thus, Tom. Under Elizabeth and now James. Have you forgotten the heads over London Bridge?" Traitors' heads were put on pikes as a warning.

"No, but-"

"-James is not like a kindly rich uncle you want to please in order to obtain some treats in return. He is the King with absolute power over all his subjects. And that," he said, fixing Tom with a rather stern expression, "includes you and me."

His tone softened a little. "If Will writes a poem, it can have life when it is spoken or when it is read. It may even have life as one of these new folios that they have started to make. But a play is different. If he writes a play and cannot perform it because of plague or lack of money or lack of a patron- or all three, then what he has written does not even exist. It is like making a cake that is never cooked and no-one eats. If we have to smile sweetly at James and indulge a few interests of his, then that we will do if that is the means by which a play is performed.

"That is the height of our ambition. What," he said tilting his head in Tom's direction, "is yours?"

Tom thought for a moment. "I just want to make my parents proud. Well, my mother really."

"And that is a worthy ambition, Tom. You have all the qualities that we are looking for. You are tall, you can read, you can act and your voice has not yet broken. And most important of all, you're not afraid of hard work. It can be difficult to live up to the expectations of your parents." There was a pause and then he continued. "Will's father rose to be Chief Bailiff in Stratford, you know. He was a very important man. But then…something happened."

"What?"

"Don't worry, he didn't kill the King. No, but he undertook some foolish business deals, especially involving money-lending and dealing in wool, both of which Elizabeth's spies used to keep a close eye on. He was fined but it was more the damage done to his reputation, which broke his spirit. He never really recovered and died about ten years ago."

"I'm…sorry." He did not know what to say.

"Tis no matter. Tis the way of things. The old must give way to the new. It's in your blood," said Ned, with a supportive hand on his shoulder. "You will always find people who doubt you, Tom. You must seek out those who believe in you too."

The weather had been poor so far that summer and the company needed some sunshine for the yard to be packed. Ned looked out from the tiring-house at a wall of black clouds marching towards them. "Unfortunately, if this weather keeps up, we will all be beggars soon."

Later, Tom was helping sweep up in the galleries and was shocked at the mess. From the tiring-house, the noblemen who sat up here looked sophisticated and superior to the groundlings down in the yard.

His head-shaking was interrupted by Will who had been sitting right at the back in his favourite spot among the shadows, watching him. "They are used to the finer things- clothes, food and-" he said, picking up an apple-core, "-servants to clean up after them. Just because someone wears a fine gown, do not assume they are a more moral person. We live in an age where we do not just act, we must be seen."

"What do you mean?"

He came forward and leaned back against the balcony, facing away from the stage, looking up into the gallery. "Look at the seats."

"What about them?"

"Look closer. It is true they have some cover from the elements and a cushion for an extra penny but there are no backs to those seats. Like those expensive so-called 'Gentleman's Places' above the stage, where the players are mostly performing while facing away from you, they don't necessarily provide the best view. The point is, anyone sitting in those places declares themselves people of some means.

"Much of the business of government is theatre, in its purest sense. Looking important is as vital as being important. Gestures are not just gestures- they can be the difference between life and death. Think Tom. Royal processions, court masques, even public executions. Every day brings more theatre into daily life. Our biggest difficulty here is to keep up."

That evening in the tavern, the company sat around a table of heavy, dark wood and talked late into the night. The apprentices, even the youngest, were there too and as the tankards of ale were emptied and refilled, it was the youngest who became the loudest.

Tom looked across at them. "Should we not say something? We do not want the landlord to throw us out."

Heminges shook his head. "They know us here. Besides," he nodded over at the apprentices. "The boys need the chance to make merry. They are not work-shy. To survive in the playhouse is to know what work is."

Eventually, after several hours of drinking and heated discussion, they were the only customers left.

Will stood and the table fell silent. "The time has come."

"To go home?" asked Tom. He was feeling guilty for enjoying himself.

"No, Tom. It is nearly the witching-hour. The time when spirits are at large. In short, tis the time…for stories. Tell us about yourself, Tom."

It was hard to laugh and joke when his mother was sitting at home alone, fretting about the future. He thought about whether to describe how his mother came to be ill or what little he knew about how his father had disappeared.

Tom had heard stories when he was growing up of The Spanish Armada, a great fleet of ships which somehow Sir Francis Drake and the English had managed to defeat. He hadn't quite understood that part of the story but he liked it when his mother described the battles at sea. She had lived for a time in Portsmouth, which was where she had met his father, who was a deck-hand when he could drag himself away from the taverns.

"We grew up poor. On good days, there was dark, rye bread and cheese on the table, washed down with ale. On less good days, on most days, there was little bread, no cheese and only water from the public pump, which often made us ill.

"We slept on beds of straw and growing up, I only had two rough tunics. That was my entire wardrobe. When I woke up, wondering what to put on for the day was not a difficult decision. One tunic was clean while the other was being washed.

"Our house is an alms-house, a special house for the poor who have done the city some service. We live there because my father was a soldier. It's tiny- we only have two rooms with a couple of small windows, so it's always dark. We are often unable to pay even the low rent and shortly before I stumbled in here, we were due to be thrown out. My coming here has saved us in many ways."

He paused becoming conscious of so many eyes upon him but he continued. "I don't remember much about my father. He…left us when I was only three but I have a dream of him and I have had these dreams so many times for so many years, I feel they must be true.

"In the dream, I am in a playhouse, a little like The Globe. I start to cry because I'm small. Everyone is bigger than me and I cannot see. And my father reaches down and lifts me up, right up, on his shoulders". In telling the story, Tom could almost put himself in the dream. "I can feel the rough hairs on his arms and his beard but I feel safe that I cannot fall and I'm taller than everyone there and I start laughing and…well, that's when I wake up." He looked around the group who were all staring at him. "It's just a foolish story."

"There are no such things," said Will, smiling.

The next day, Edmund was given the role of prompt. This was far from ideal but having caused problems wherever he was, Will calculated it was the best way to keep him out of trouble. He was wrong.

Midway through Lady Macbeth's big speech where she calls upon evil powers, Tom became flustered and nervous and called for a prompt. Unfortunately the word that Edmund called out was wrong and would have led Tom down a blind alley. Luckily he extemporised and the audience didn't even notice.

Will however, certainly did.

After the performance, Tom was full of apologies but it was not Tom to whom Will wished to speak. "What happened?" he snapped at Edmund. "With the line?"

"I, er, lost my place."

"Yes, you have. Now go and help sweep the stage. We have strict rules here. Rules about attendance, punctuality and doing a job properly. If you cannot do your job, we cannot pay you. This is your one and only warning. Fail again and you must leave."

Will had delivered all this in a very calm and measured tone but Tom could see Edmund's face turn as pale as the grey ash spread about the yard and did as he was bid without a further word.

Chapter Eleven
How to Kill a King

'If it were done when tis done,
then t'were well it were done quickly.'
(*Macbeth*, I, (vii), l. 1-2)

Ned was controlling the tiring-room area, still with pins in his mouth, a quill in his hand for late changes and in quiet moments, of which there were few, he crossed over to a chess board set up on a stool in the corner and made a move against an imaginary opponent.

Tom watched in admiration, struggling with his single task-mending a shirt that Edmund had somehow managed to rip on one arm. "How can you do that?"

"It's alright, so long as I don't swallow."

"No, I don't mean the pins, I mean…" He gestured towards the chess-board.

"Oh, I see. It helps me stay calm."

Will was brooding in a corner, without a quill in hand, which was unusual. "What is the matter?" Although Tom was a relative newcomer, he felt emboldened to ask. The company worked through mutual respect and a principle that if you were good enough, you were old enough.

Will threw the quill down in frustration. "It's the banquet scene. Have you finished with this?" He gestured to the chessboard and Ned waved him on. He began to move chess-pieces into the position of characters on stage. "The seating is all important- see? That is where the noblemen sit, the Macbeths are at the head of the table and there is the seat which Banquo's ghost could use." He pointed at his elaborate design like a general planning a battle. "When Lady Macbeth says, 'You know your own degrees' she is trying to make all the order of society appear natural and in its rightful place. By the end, even she cannot keep people in their places and the meeting breaks up. She cannot contain the devils in her husband's mind or indeed as we discover later, her own."

"So what's the problem?"

"We don't have a player for the ghost. Everyone is on the stage except the witches and they need time for a costume change."

"Why not…?" began Tom but his voice trailed off.

"What?"

"Oh, nothing."

"No, go on. Speak." He sounded a little like Macbeth commanding the witches.

"Well, perchance Macbeth can speak to…thin air." Tom had been bemused initially by Will's description of the witches 'vanishing into thin air' but now he felt comfortable enough to use the phrase himself.

"Thin air?" repeated Will.

"Yes. See, I told you it was foolish."

"No, go on."

"Well, he could address an empty chair. That could be the ghost."

Ned scoffed. "The crowd will howl, Will. They will expect blood and a proper ghost. Come on, Tom. Let's leave Will in peace." He began to usher Tom away.

"Stay," commanded Will. He lowered his voice. "Let the boy stay. He may have something."

"Lice probably," muttered Edmund, who was taking a break from sweeping in order to eavesdrop near the back of the stage.

Tom came back. "So what of the blood, boy?"

"Well, every time Macbeth sees the ghost, his appearance changes slightly. The power of the scene is in the words. You told me that. We can see the wounds on Banquo because of the way Macbeth describes them. The crowd must use their…mind's eye." Another phrase from *Hamlet*. "It makes sense too because he is the only one who can see the ghost. And the dagger earlier- well, that's only proceeding from his diseased mind, isn't it? A false creation," he added, using a phrase from Macbeth's speech to the airborne dagger that draws him on to kill the King.

There was a long pause, during which Will stared long at Tom before eventually declaring, "Come with me. I would speak further with you." The pair moved to Will's desk at the far end of the tiring-house in hotly-animated conversation, leaving Edmund looking after them, his hands balling into a fist.

"Now," continued Will, picking up a quill. "When Banquo challenges the witches and says 'If you can look into the seeds of time,' that is an important question. James has traced his lineage back to the real historical figure of Banquo."

"I did not know that," admitted Tom, a little shocked.

"Some knowledge can be useful. James claims that he can trace his family further back than any other European King. The play also shows the establishment of the right of first-born sons in Scotland. It does make your idea with Banquo's ghost a little better too as we will not be looking directly at one of James' distant relatives, covered in blood.

"That's also why it's a good idea for Banquo to remain loyal and true to his principles. He doubts the words of the witches. Indeed he seeks to warn Macbeth that 'the instruments of darkness often tell us truths, win us with honest trifles' and then betray us whereas Macbeth swallows them like a greedy trout at the end of a line. It is also why," he continued, "Banquo does not promise to support Macbeth no matter what he does and I have even penned a few lines in which Macbeth wishes he were more like Banquo."

"You mean the 'under him, my genius is rebuked,' part?"

"Exactly!" He clapped Tom on the back, almost knocking him over. "You are a natural player, Tom. And the chronicles mention diseased folk seeking the touch of the King, believing it will cure them. Tis a power James thinks he has inherited from Edward the Confessor."

"And do you believe that?"

"It is enough that he believes it. I shall insert a line or two about

Macbeth being a disease which needs a cure. He will make the connection."

"But is it true?"

"Like all stories, Tom, if people believe it, then it is true." He paused a moment. "Then there is the question of how your character dies."

"Must she die?"

Will chuckled, which seemed odd given the subject of their talk. "This is a tragedy, Tom. Lady Macbeth has prompted her husband not just to the act of murder but to kill the King- there is no worse crime. She must die- the question is how. She cannot die in battle. Such scenes can be powerful in history plays but there are always difficulties in making the mass of people believe such things. She would not lack stomach for the fight but as a woman, she would not be allowed. She could be poisoned but I have used that before with Gertrude in *Hamlet*."

"Why can't she kill herself?"

"That too is in *Hamlet*." It seemed to Tom as if the world was in *Hamlet*.

"But in that play," observed Tom, "the hero only talks about self-murder. Here, she has such evil in her and she-" he struggled to find the words and resorted instead to gestures- "it is like she pushes her true nature down and down but that truth must ultimately…explode like a…volcano. She turns mad."

"And yet we only have a few scenes so each time we see her, she must change. It will be hard. You have rehearsed your part and have learned your lines. You know where this story leads but the crowd-" he made a sweeping gesture out towards the empty seats- "they, do not. A very few may have scratches and patches from Holinshed's Chronicles but as for written history, known and measured- that is little more than stories. Vague stories that a mother might tell a curious child. Still, it is of no consequence. This is a playhouse, not a schoolhouse.

"As for Lady Macbeth, her death, the sleepwalking- this is all but conjecture." He gave a rare sigh of satisfaction. "She is one of my finest creations. She is the utmost evil, prepared to commit murder and not just any murder but that of the anointed King. And yet-" he paused and stared out towards the stage as if lost in thought for a moment.

"And yet?" continued Tom.

"And yet she loves her husband. She would damn both their souls for the chance of glory here on earth. And she does it with grace and wit and…charm. The charm of a snake that enchants just before it strikes. That is what you must be, Tom." His expression must have suggested his concern. "Do you think you should never do what disturbs your soul?"

"No, but-"

"-In my plays, I try to take people on a journey. It may not be one they would normally choose but like any journey, one of the reasons to travel is to see new things. And possibly be changed by the experience. If you do not wish to take this adventure, you should stay at home. But," he added with a twinkle in his eye, "You will miss out on all the fun."

"Have I changed?"

Will looked at Tom like a merchant assessing the price of an unusual item. "Only you can answer that. Here." He handed him a prop.

"A candle?"

"Of course. It's very important for you. Most of your scenes are at night, the sleepwalking one most obviously. She cannot sleep any more than her husband as her mind is turning. We must mark the hour and make the crowd believe it is night-time."

"I will manage."

"I'm sure you will. That still leaves how exactly?"

"Well," said Tom. "She was on the battlements to call upon the spirits of evil and to drug the guards so perchance she could return there. And fall."

"Hmm. We could use the tiring-house but we couldn't see the actual fall. We cannot risk physical injury to our cast." This wasn't sentiment but the cold, hard reality of performing six shows a week.

The balcony was used for scenes like the *Romeo and Juliet* declaration of love but it could also represent the battlements of Macbeth's castle.

Tom pressed on. "At the right moment, I could hurry down the internal stairwell in one of the turrets on the edge of the stage and while Burbage is giving one of his big speeches, I could position myself on the ground, legs and arms splayed out awkwardly as if from a fall."

A smile slowly crossed Will's face. "You are a great one for problems, Tom. It was indeed a lucky day for us when you appeared amongst us. Out of thin air."

Suddenly, there was a violent rumble of thunder. The weather had not been kind so far that season and Tom instinctively looked out through the traverse but there were no dark clouds in the sky. Then he realised the noise was coming from behind and above him, from within the huts to be precise. There, he later learned, Cuthbert was rolling some cannon balls in a box. It was a simple enough idea but very effective.

Will wrote about two new plays a year so most of the productions were of older work or by authors other than himself, like Marlowe and Jonson. Thus it was that while they were working on *Macbeth*, the company also decided to bring back a crowd-pleaser from a few seasons earlier, *Hamlet*. However this created problems of its own.

Burbage took a break from rehearsals and stuck his head round the drape of the tiring-house. Will would sometimes 'borrow' Tom's desk for some quick scribbling if he had an idea he wanted to write down there and then. The place was a mess. There were quills and ink everywhere, so-called 'foul papers' or first drafts strewn across the table and most of the floor.

There were also a few sharp knives hanging from a nail on the back wall. Goose feathers lasted a while but Will was writing so many hours of the day, they all became blunt eventually.

Burbage was aware of the importance of the moment and so waited until the scratching of Will's nib fell silent.

"May I crave a word, Will?"

"As many as you wish," replied the writer, who had noted Burnage's appearance and appreciated the pause.

He entered and stood rather awkwardly, taking the hat from his head and passing the brim through his hands, in a needless gesture.

"It's just that…"

"That what?"

"These long speeches…"

"What of them?"

"Well, do we…really need them?"

Will smiled. "I know they can be hard to learn. Remember, I too am a player. And it is a challenge to hold the attention of an audience sometimes but in such places there is also some of my best work. Ideas, thoughts, poetry- it's all there." He paused and tried to think of a way to express this simply. "It is like seeing right into their mind. In such speeches, characters never lie."

"Never?" Tom had chipped in, despite intending to remain quiet and listen

He shook his head. "And they speak to the audience as if they were conversing with a friend. For they have no-one else in the play to talk to. Indeed, that is why they speak. We are being told secrets that no-one else knows. Sometimes they are working out a problem or just trying to understand their own feelings. Do you never talk to yourself when you're alone?"

Tom had to admit he did. Indeed, before he joined the company, his only conversations were whispered conversations with himself in the dark at the end of the day.

"The thing is, Will," Burbage continued, "this play-"

"-*Hamlet*?"

"Yes, *Hamlet*. It's good. Make no mistake. Ghosts, murder, suicide, a pile of bodies- it's all very well but I'm wondering if there isn't a bit…too much of it."

"Too much?"

"It looks like it will run well over four hours. The last time we had a play that long, the crowd ended up relieving themselves on the stage."

"Maybe they just didn't like the play."

"Hmm. The thing is…I was wondering if we might…trim some of these lines?"

"Trim?"

Will's tone had suddenly gone icy but Burbage pressed on. "Just a few. A little trim, here and there. Just some of the more…troublesome lines."

"Hmm." He looked up. "I'll see what I can do. I can probably snip a soliloquy a little."

"It may take more than that, Will. We need to try and finish with some daylight. And why does the main character disappear for so long?"

"It is a demanding role, Burbage. You may well need a rest."

"Well, it could be all of us that will be having a nice long rest if no-one wants to come and spend the last years of their life sitting through *Hamlet*."

"Or standing," chipped in Tom.

"And you, boy," said Will, throwing him a glance which told him not to forget his place in the greater scheme of things, "won't be able to sit if I have booted your scrawny hams out of this place. Perhaps long after I'm dead, someone will make all of this into a book, even the extra scenes."

There was a pause and then laughter as they realised it was only a joke.

As usual, Will said a few words to the company before the performance. Today, it was a blend of inspiration and warning. "Lest we forget," he declared, looking around the main cast, squeezed into the tiring-room, "we are not the only playhouse in town. If the groundlings do not like what we serve them, they will go to The Fortune or perhaps even The Rose." He did however give an instinctive wrinkling of the nose even at the name of the latter venue that had been built on marshland and had retained the damp and dank smell of what lay beneath the boards. "Henslowe, the owner," he added by way of explanation for Tom, "he even has a frame to give the illusion of beheading a man. I'm told it's quite spectacular."

"Why don't we do that?" asked Tom, a bit too enthusiastically.

"We must do what we do best. To thine own self be true."

"And what's that?"

"Not tricks. We deal in a different kind of magic. We must use the tools at our disposal- words." He turned back to the group. "Anyway, what I wanted to say was that tomorrow, I must away to Stratford. It is two days' hard ride. I will return before Sunday but I have business I must attend to. It is a trifling matter. I have investments in land and property and need sometimes to take recourse to the law to make sure no-one is stealing from me. Anyway, I shall be thinking of you."

The gathering broke up and Will began to put his papers together. He would undoubtedly do some writing when he could even on a journey of this nature.

Tom watched him for a while as the final player left the room. "Do you think of Stratford often?"

He nodded. "It is never far from my thoughts."

"And yet none of the plays mention it?"

"Oh, they do." Tom frowned- he must double-check. He'd managed to read some others from a handwritten pile of notes. "But-" he began.

"-Much of my boyhood was spent in the Forests of Arden in Warwickshire. I'm a country-boy at heart. The trees and plants, the birds of the field, the names for the equipment used to hunt- these are all familiar to me. If I wish to make a comparison, it is entirely natural that it should come from that part of my life. Anyway, look after the company for me, Tom."

"Me?"

"Yes, you are one of us now."

Rehearsals and performances proceeded as planned and Will returned several days later. After only a few minutes of the first rehearsal, he noticed something was different and began scrabbling frantically through sheets of paper in the tiring-house before striding out to the stage.

"Who wrote this line?" he demanded loudly. There was a silence. "Speak, who wrote this?" No-one wanted to put their head on the block. Slowly Tom raised his hand. "You?"

"You were away and we needed the sides. I read the rest of the play. I know it better than anyone here. I talked with Burbage and the others and, well….yes, I wrote it."

"It's…good. Middleton will want his name on them but we will know the real Thomas behind the witches."

Armin's Porter's scene was a crowd favourite. It was really there to allow Burbage, as Macbeth, to wash the stage-blood from his hands and change his clothes but it also allowed Armin to show his comic talents- which were considerable. To be honest, when Tom had first read the play, full of grisly murders and the capital crime of killing the King, he wasn't sure that he wanted to even finish reading it. The world that Will wrote about and the way that it came alive on stage had given Tom several nightmares. He wasn't sure about witches- at least, he'd never seen one but there were so many things in life that couldn't be explained, it made as much sense as anything else. Worse than the witches, was the idea of killing the King. Tom had always been brought up to know his place in the world. If it was possible to kill a King, then the very fabric of the social world around him could be turned upside down. They'd be saying next that the world wasn't flat or that bleeding the sick didn't help them.

He took a deep breath to try and dispel such dark thoughts and immediately wished he hadn't. Most days, it would be fair to say that the crowd, especially in the yard, produced quite a stench. Noblemen smoked clay pipes and carried pomanders filled with lavender, rosemary, sage and other sweet-smelling herbs designed to cloak the odour. These latter objects were often worn at the waist on a chain, so that they could be swung to and fro like a priest hoping to cast out something especially sinful. There were always a certain number of people coughing in the audience. Any gathering of that number was never going to be silent but it seemed particularly bad today.

Armin stomped into the tiring-house, having played his scene which normally brought the house down. "Why do people come to the playhouse just to cough their lungs out?" he snapped, prompting a forefinger-to-lips gesture from Tom. This may be the great Robert Armin but the hangings in front of the tiring-house were thin and more to block sight than sound. Ned was sat on a stool nearby, concentrating hard, sewing a number of tiny pearls onto a pair of leather gloves.

"Hmm," said Armin, unimpressed. "If they don't want to listen to my voice out there, I hardly think they'll pay much attention to it from here."

It was dark. The rest of the company had gone home and Tom was the last one, as often was the case, doing a final tidy up. He was sweeping the stage with one of the brooms used by the Witches as a prop to show their status. Tom actually felt it was unnecessary but Edmund wanted to have one. He was always very keen to have any props or costumes available- basically anything for him to play with and draw the audience's attention while he was on stage.

At the sight of a flickering candle, he poked his head through the drapes of the tiring-house.

Will was crouched over a desk, totally immersed in his work and unaware of Tom's presence or probably, even that night had fallen.

He gave a small cough, so as not to startle Will, who looked up.

"Ah, Tom. Nearly done. Just tying up…one or two loose ends."

One of the foul papers began to move on its own. Tom lurched backwards, crashing into some swords laid ready for the following day's performance, which fell to the floor with a clatter. He pointed. "Tis…tis a devil." He was gasping for breath and staring madly as the paper continued to move without anyone touching it.

Will, on the other hand, remained perfectly unruffled and looked up at Tom with some amusement. "Calm yourself, Tom. Tis no devil. See."

He leant over and lifted a page or two to reveal a large black and white…rat. It was only Lucius.

"Aghhh." Tom was relieved there was no supernatural presence but if he was honest, he was no great fan of rats either. At home, they had some up on the roof at times and they used to keep him awake. He used to have nightmares about them burying through the roof and falling on his face.

"Oh, by the way, I've given you a small part in what I'm working on now."

"In *King Lear*?"

"Well, in a way. The character of Edgar pretends at one point to be mad and he adopts the role of a mad beggar called Tom."

"Is that how you see me? A mad beggar?"

"No but until your voice deepens and you grow a little more, you may have to content yourself with such nods and winks. Besides," he added, a little more seriously, "sometimes you have to go a little mad in order to stay sane."

Tom was in the middle of answering, when a small apprentice came sprinting into the room. "I think you'd better come and look at this, Will," he gasped.

"What is it?"

"Just come and see." Will reluctantly put his papers down and, taking a candle to illuminate the way in the fading light, followed the younger boy, along with Tom, out of the main gate and round the building towards London Bridge.

"There," said the little fellow, pointing. A notice had been unceremoniously nailed to the wall of the playhouse that faced the public thoroughfare.

"What does it say?" asked Tom.

"How should I know?" the boy squeaked. Tom forgot sometimes that not everyone could read.

"Alright, let me have a look." He pushed his way through past a small crowd that had gathered to read the notice. I'm sure it's n-"

He froze in midsentence. The word at the top of the bill leaped out at him and sent a chill through his blood but he managed to read it aloud: "'CLOSED- By order of the Master of the Revels. Due to plague conditions, this playhouse shall remain closed until further notice. Occupants are advised to avoid contact with contaminated persons or vermin such as mice or…'" His voice trailed off.

He looked across at Will in shock and horror. And then he yelled the one word that flashed into his mind. "NED!!"

Chapter Twelve

The Hand of Death

'A plague on both your houses.'
(*Romeo & Juliet*, III, (i), l. 106)

Tom hammered at the door of Ned's hovel that he shared with three other families. A man, wearing a scarf tied over face, opened the front door but held up a firm hand to prevent entry. Above the mask, Tom could see two grey, watery eyes that looked like they'd seen something that normal people shouldn't see. His breathing was raspy and he looked far from healthy. "It is the fever," he whispered feebly.

"But-" began Tom.

"-There can be no doubt," the man cut in. This must be Ned's uncle. His friend had spoken of his kindness but there was little charity in his eyes, just soulless resignation. "Ned has a great fever and when he can speak, talks of chills and headaches. He sleeps most of the time but his neck, armpits and legs all are swollen. Apart from seeking to cool his fever, there is little we can do for him."

"Can't I see him for a minute?"

The man shook his head firmly. "He recognises no-one and has begun to vomit blood. He is covered with buboes, huge great red things and has convulsions and knows not where he is. If it does not reach his lungs, then he has a chance." He would not meet Tom's eyes directly, suggesting he didn't really believe this.

"So there is hope?"

The man sighed. "We have done what we can- checked his urine and given him some powdered earthworm." Tom grimaced. He knew

126

medicine often didn't taste nice but he was never convinced by the idea that the worst it tasted, the more effective it was. "There's always hope, I suppose. But for now, prayer is all that I can recommend." He closed the door.

Three days later, news reached them that was not entirely unexpected but still came as something of a shock. The speed with which it first showed itself, developed symptoms and the person concerned died- all that could pass in a matter of a few days. It was terrifying.

Will came and put an arm round Tom's shoulders, which began to shake uncontrollably. After a while, the tears stopped. Still neither of them spoke. Eventually, Tom pushed Will's arm away and ran out.

Heminges made to follow him but Will held up a hand. "Let him go."

A while later, Will found Tom sitting by the river. Across on the other side, smoke rose from the burning of plague bodies which had already begun.

Will sat down next to him. "Death stalks us throughout our lives, Tom. You know that. There are so many things from childbirth onwards from which medicine cannot protect us. So many poxes of differing kinds, typhus, ague, even before we talk of plague." He shuddered. "The outbreaks in 1592 and 1603, each wiped out about a quarter of the population of the entire city.

"And even if we are spared disease, a quarrel, maybe not of our making, can lead to daggers being drawn. I'm sure Marlowe thought he had many years ahead of him. My fellow poet Ben Jonson was almost hung in 1598 for killing a player in a duel. In a way, I was lucky that Marlowe died when he did."

"Lucky?"

"We were born in the same year, you know, Tom. 1564. He worked for our main rival, Edward Alleyn, and the Lord Admiral's Men at The Rose. In 93 when he died, he had already created *Tamburlaine the Great*, *The Jew of Malta* and the great *Dr Faustus*- in short, more works of note than I. Had he lived, who knows what more he might have produced. It could have been me taken so pointlessly or it could have been him who went on to become famous. It's just a matter of fate."

Neither of them spoke for a while. Then Will continued as if there had been no pause. "And even if we are not fearful of death for ourselves, it still holds us. We actively seek it out in our entertainment, watching bears or dogs in baiting pits or criminals being publically executed at Tyburn. How many men over 50 do you know?" It was perhaps an odd question to throw at a 13-year-old but Tom knew what he meant. "This life is too brief- something which I failed to recognise as a younger man but now I come to realise all too well. You know, Tom. I had two younger sisters." Tom shook his head. He did not. "Joan and Margaret. I never knew them. They both died before I was born. I was the first Shakespeare to survive my first year of life." He sighed at Tom's black look. "What I'm trying to say is, death is always there, sometimes just an observer in the background but sometimes an active player in our lives. Perhaps I lead a charmed life."

"You sound like a Puritan."

"Maybe they are not wrong about everything. But we cannot let death rule our lives. We must live. It is our dilemma, shared by no other animal- they do not know they are mortal."

Tom wasn't entirely sure about this. He'd known dogs who had limped into a corner to die and they seemed to know the end was near.

"If we were immortal, there would be nothing precious about Beauty because it would always be there. We appreciate Beauty in nature because we know it will not last forever. So must we be with people. There is no time for anything else. I left school at 15. Married at 18. Nothing perhaps unusual in that but I wanted to make my mark upon the world and was in a hurry to get to it. Being a thrice-times father before I was 20, well, let's just say that did not help."

"How many children do you have?"

"Two."

Tom frowned. "I thought Ned said you had-"

"-One died." There was an awkward pause. "Hamnet. My son. He…died."

"I'm…" He didn't really know what he was… "Sorry."

"That's alright, Tom." Will took a deep breath. "Many suffer loss. In times of plague, whole families, towns even are wiped from the earth. I try not to brood on it but sometimes, it happens. Hamnet died in 96. Stratford has felt a good deal colder since and Anne and I…well, let's just say, there have been greater love-matches. She was already 26 when we married. I was only just 18," he added. "You are still young in the ways of the world. Marriage does not always bring the happiness one expects." He looked out across the city for a moment and his expression clouded over.

"Hamnet would be…21 by now. A man. He was very like me-headstrong and often the cause of arguments." He looked at Tom in a slightly strange way. "I see something of him in you. He too was tall for his age and carried himself with a bit of a stoop as if no-one would notice. He worried about what others said about him and would take himself off on his own at times. What people never consider when they have children is what it means for later life."

"Someone to visit and care for you, you mean?"

He threw back his head and roared with laughter. "No, you young fool. Think of the huge pile of money that you could have to support you in your frail, old age were it not for school fees, debts at the alehouse or with an angry landlord."

"Do you really think that? Is there no joy in being a father?"

"Sometimes." His face clouded over. "But children can be a vale of tears."

"And yet you are successful now?"

"As it turned out, things took a little longer than I had hoped but we seem to be moderately successful now, yes. But do not imagine all is calm. It is like a swan who may float serenely along a river but whose legs beneath the surface are industry itself. Here in London, there are rivalries between public and private playhouses- the private ones are inside the city limits and generally attract a better quality customer- between different companies of boy players, especially the choirs St Paul's and the Chapel Royal, even between players in the same company. Even here in the playhouse, there are still social divisions between people. So-called 'sharers' like myself pay all the bills and take such profits as there are. 'Hired men' are paid weekly and then at the bottom of the heap are the apprentices- boys learning the trade as well as playing all the female parts. It only seems as if we're all one happy family when viewed from outside."

Tom nodded. "Just like real families then."

"Why don't you go home? There'll be no performance today." Or for the foreseeable future, he thought grimly.

Tom nodded and walked off but he soon realised that he couldn't go straight home. What could he tell his mother? That he'd been lying to her for weeks and that the dream that he'd been living was now over? He crossed the bridge into the city and wandered along one of the dark, narrow streets in Cheapside. He glanced up but could only make out a chink of sky between the roofs above, which jutted out into the street, further and further with each floor so that they almost touched at the top.

He came out by the river again and stumbled along in a daze, not paying attention to where his feet led him. The streets were filthy as always and waste ran straight into the Thames. Looking down into the water, there were still fish visible but Tom sometimes wondered for how long.

There were regular outbreaks of plague every few years. Public gatherings of any kind were banned. The playhouses that the Puritans saw as hotbeds of vice even when there was no plague, were forced to close when more than 30 people died in a single week. It was a bad time to be an actor. There might be some work to be had as a travelling player, performing in tavern courtyards but there was no guarantee of a steady income.

The last major plague outbreak had been only three years earlier. It was so dangerous that the new King stayed out of the city until the following year. Tom had strong memories of carts arriving every night to collect bodies from neighbouring houses. Several front doors had big red crosses daubed on them and the inhabitants were forbidden to leave until the fever had passed. He had helped by passing some bread through a window to a boy he used to play with but whose breathless thanks were the last he ever heard of him. There was no time for individual burial. The carts took corpses to giant communal pits outside the city, filled with lime to help speed the process of decomposition.

Nobles and well-to-do people left the city as soon as they could, leaving the poorest to their fate. Some tried to wear face-masks, others carried pomanders and fires were lit in the belief that this purified the air. In truth, this seemed to have little effect and within a few short days, the neighbourhood he had grown up in was devastated with about every fifth house lying empty.

Looking back across at the bridge, he spied the Church of St Mary's Ovaries and thought of the advice Ned's uncle had given him but couldn't bring himself to enter. Religion hadn't played a big part in his life, except from those who would judge and condemn him, first as a beggar, then later as a player.

He had been surrounded by death all his life like any other Londoner and he had seen the effects of plague before but Ned had been special. He was one of the welcoming voices that had accepted him into the world of the playhouse and who had taught him so much. A great wave of gratitude welled up inside him and as hot tears poured down his cheeks, he vowed to make the most of the chance he had been given.

Chapter Thirteen

A Plan of Action

'Wisely and slow. They stumble that run fast.'
(*Romeo and Juliet,* II (iii), l. 90)

The key members of the company and Tom had gathered in The Tabard Inn. Will got to his feet and surveyed the faces round the table with a serious and sober expression.

"Well, gentlemen, I have not called you together to become maudlin about the past. I have an announcement." The company fell silent.

"Due to the closure of The Globe, we must go on a tour." There were some groans. "Yes, I know but we have no choice. Back in 92 remember, we had to close for nearly two years."

"TWO YEARS!" exclaimed Tom.

"It was why I took to longer poems for a while. Don't worry, we'll manage. Anyway, I have some news. We already have one interested party. Quite an important one." He paused, deliberately dragging out the moment.

"Well, don't leave us waiting, Will," said Cuthbert. "Who is it?"

"The King. He wishes to see a performance of *Macbeth*. Just for him and some specially-invited guests." Tom, who had been fetching more ale, sat down with a bit of a thump. "Including...his brother-in-law, King Christian V of Denmark." There was a gasp or two. "Now, don't worry, they say he speaks scarcely a word of English."

"James?"

"No, Edmund. I'm talking about the Danish King."

"Won't that make it difficult to please him?" asked Cuthbert.

"There will be a banquet beforehand and he will probably will be merry enough-" he mimed the action of drinking a goblet of wine "-by the time the play starts."

"When do we perform?" asked Burbage, considering practical matters.

Will paused again. "Next Monday."

"Next Monday! But…but…it's Wednesday today."

"It could be worse."

"How?"

"Well, considering the presence of the Danish King, we might have been rehearsing *Hamlet*."

By the following day, Cuthbert had done a deal with Harry, the portly, silver-haired Landlord to allow them to use the Tabard Inn as a base for rehearsal. For his part, the man had willingly agreed to keep them supplied with food and drink. He was very glad of every last penny he could get. The loss of The Globe was going to hit his business hard.

"Right," said Cuthbert. "There's no time to waste. I have a job for you, Tom." He handed him a sheaf of papers.

Tom looked at the first one. "*Macbeth*. What do you wish me to do?"

"Read through this and remove any reference to God, Jesus or the Holy Ghost or all three."

"Why?"

"Why? Do you live under a rock, boy? By Act of Parliament passed but two months hence, if we fail to do so, we may face a fine of ten pounds. That is for each actor on every occasion. We could be ruined. So get your quill out and be quick about it!"

"Will will not be pleased."

"Will is never pleased. But it is a choice between obeying this law and being a beggar in the street. Do you wish to return to your old life?"

Tom got to work without another word.

Later, Will passed by and Tom had still not finished. From his huffing and puffing, all did not seem well.

"I assume this angers you too. If others limit the words you can use, I mean."

Will shook his head. "Actually, the reverse is true." He could see from Tom's expression that he could not understand. "Think, Tom. I dare say you have heard fellows in the street and perhaps even here within these walls use words which they should not. All words have power, Tom. Some more than others and we should weigh them carefully. A mouth that spews nothing but profanities has little guiding intelligence. Do animals swear? No. They do their business without fuss and we must do the same.

"My good friend, Mr Jonson fills his plays with references to the body and there are characters in my work who insult and curse but not without just cause. In addition, we may never know who is listening. There are Puritan spies everywhere. If we use profanities, we can be fined or even closed. I am no Puritan, I think you know that Tom but if their rules force us to use more creative language, then they do us a service and I for one, am grateful."

The following day, Tom was rehearsing with Burbage. "What's he like?" asked Tom.

"Who? James? Well, he's…the King." Considering the company had played many times at his 'request,' that wasn't quite the detailed answer that Tom was hoping for.

"James has achieved a measure of good. The country is more unified north and south of the border and the strife with Catholics seems a little calmer. We are not at war with a foreign power and as James has children, the question of succession is more settled than for years. Maybe he had a measure of luck, but he caught the Gunpowder plotters and he is even having a union flag designed, a 'Jack' so they say."

"A what!" cried Tom in alarm. The name still had the potential to scare him.

"A Jack. A Union Jack. It's the name of the flag."

"Oh, right."

Burbage gave Tom a bit of a stare. He had proved his worth to the company many times and yet he could still occasionally blurt out something that was a bit strange.

"Historians will probably say this was the first performance but history is written by the rich and influential."

"Won't the King be displeased if he hears the play has been performed to ordinary folk before him?"

"I think he will be more displeased if our performance is rough-edged and lacking the polish of practice. No, we have had lord chamberlains visit us before and they always emphasise the need to make the performance for the King of the highest quality. How better to do that than practice? We must take care not to displease the King. These are changing times."

"How do you mean?"

Burbage sighed at Tom's naivety. "Let me explain something. About five years ago, you'd be no more than a young boy then but what do you remember of Essex?"

"He was a traitor."

"Exactly. The Earl of Essex and several other prominent members of the aristocracy plotted to overthrow the Queen and put in her place the Catholic, Mary. They planned a grand rebellion here in London and what was to be the spark of such an uprising?" Tom had no idea. "A performance right here of *Richard II*. The removal of the King featured in the play was meant to stir up such passions that the people would march on The Royal Palace and seize power."

"So what happened?" Tom's eyes were bright with eager anticipation.

"Well, we, as The Lord's Chamberlain's Men as we were then, agreed to perform the play- we could hardly afford to say no. And at the time, we did not realise the scope of Essex's ambition. The performance went ahead, the play was well-received but there was no spontaneous outpouring of hatred for Elizabeth. Instead, people stayed in their homes and Essex's rebellion was cut down by soldiers, the ringleaders arrested, tortured and eventually executed.

"Robert Catesby had been a supporter but not one of the central conspirators and was ultimately let off. Four years later, he tried to create his own plot, 'The Gunpowder Treason Plot.' His father, William, is a distant relative of Will's actually." Tom stared in amazement. "He and Robert met a couple of time as children, I believe."

"And that didn't frighten you? That the government would find some sort of link between Will and Catesby."

"But there is no link."

A thought struck Tom. "Is it possible that the plotters met here?"

"That Catesby, Fawkes and the others used the size and noise of the crowd to disguise their muttered words? Possible I suppose. It wouldn't be my first choice as a meeting place. There are lots of people but the King's spies are also everywhere and in a crowd of groundlings, they could press right up close without much warning."

"What happened to Catesby this time?"

"He was no better a plotter than Essex and sent a warning letter to friends in Parliament to leave that place before the bombs planted by Fawkes and others, were detonated. He wasn't with the others inside Parliament itself as the key arrests were made but later apprehended after a fierce exchange of gunfire in his family home. A few short days later, he was not only hung but also decapitated and his head stuck on display opposite Parliament as if his sightless eyes had to look at the object of his failed plot."

Tom could see the horrible logic of doing this, to make a public example and deter others but he was never sure that it worked. Death was just part of life for most people. He knew that public executions were very popular but could not bring himself to see it as entertainment. The hanging was bad enough but sometimes the prisoners were 'hung, drawn and quartered,' meaning they were cut down from the scaffold while still alive, stretched in some way and then disembowelled, so that their internal organs were removed and burned in front of them before they died. After decapitation, the heads were usually boiled, decorated with some ivy and placed on pikes at the southern entrance to London Bridge, which all those who crossed the bridge were forced to witness. Tom had to admit it, Kings knew how to keep hold of power.

Tom looked across to The Tower, which usually meant torture

and death for anyone taken there and shuddered. He could see a little better now why Will was concerned to court a certain element of popularity. It was all very well to be an independent artist but this was not much help if you were swinging at the end of a noose.

Later, Tom was looking through the props cupboard in the tiring-house and came upon a rather important item. Looking round furtively to check the coast was clear, he popped the crown on his head and stood in front of the full-length mirror used to check that costumes were fitted correctly.

"King Tom I, I presume?" asked Will who had appeared silently behind him.

"No, no. Well, er, perhaps," replied Tom, startled. He took it off. Although it was only a toy, he felt ashamed for having been caught.

A question struck him. "Why are Kings so important to you? I mean, so many of your plays are about them. *Richard II, Richard III, Henry VI-*" he had forgotten how many parts there were of that- "*Henry IV*, parts one and two and *Henry V*.

Will took up his habitual position at his writing table. "Shortly after he became King, James called us before him and declared, 'From this moment forward, you shall be known as The King's Men. And King's Men you shall be.'"

He gave Tom a knowing smile. "James is fully aware of the level of protection such a title gives the company. With royal approval, we can legally deck ourselves out in four-and-a-half yards of scarlet cloth provided by the crown and present ourselves as gentlemen both here in The Globe and on tour if the need arises. However," Will added. "He also knows that something has to be given in return.

"The crowds like to see how the rich and famous live. It means we can have elegant costumes, dances, feasts and for a couple of hours, when we watch a play, we too can live as Kings." He paused, gathering his thoughts. Tom had seen him do this countless times but it was still amazing to watch, like a wave drawing back slowly before unleashing its full force upon the shore.

"Kings are like our best selves. They are how we could be if we too were high-born. Weak, frail, capable of great good or evil but often just struggling. Kings must…" He sought the right words. "They must hold the nation together. In times of war, they must fight. In times of peace, they must avoid war.

"When the Chorus asks in *Henry V*, 'Can this cockpit,' meaning the playhouse,'" he explained with a sweep of his arm, "'hold the vastie fields of France?' The answer must be 'Yes'. And the only method at my disposal? Words. We do not have hundreds of players. We cannot create the real elements of conflict. But we can get to its very essence. England has fought many wars in ages past and will probably fight many more. War is a terrible thing and will be waged for reasons of profit and corruption but there are also just wars, wars of principle which must be fought. In war, we are truly tested. It is only then that we learn about our true selves."

Tom had not seen Will quite so passionate before. "Have you fought in war, Will?"

He did not answer at first and remained staring into the distance as if hearing other voices like a dog turning its head to a distant sound. At length, these voices appeared to fade and he turned back to Tom, to only partially answer the question. "My weapons are the quill and my arms are the words spoken by players.

"It is hard for you perhaps to understand. Elizabeth was on the throne so long, it seemed like she was there forever but all the while there have been those who would plot against her."

"You mean the Spaniards?"

"Yes but not only them. The French, perhaps. But not just countries. She had no heir. No children," he added.

"Why is that important?"

"It means no-one knew what would happen when she died. There was…uncertainty. And if there is one thing that rich men hate, it is uncertainty. She had whole networks of spies watching the every move of those she distrusted. Many would plot against her. They faded while she remained. She was an amazing woman.

"For much of the last twenty years, England has been at war with Catholic Spain. My plays are not really about war as such but the need for order and a strong leader. That's partly why James likes them. Elizabeth certainly enjoyed plays but James is even keener- by the end of the season, he will have seen over a dozen performances."

"Really? Here?"

"No. Monarchs tend to prefer us to go to whichever Royal Palace best suits them. Essex thought you could use plays to easily manipulate the people but they are not like small children." Will smiled. "If I write a play about witches, set in Scotland in which those who rise up against the King are severely-punished, I think James, formerly James VI of Scotland remember, only a few short months after the Gunpowder Plotters have been executed, should be very pleased.

"It's a great honour for the company to play before the King but it also gives James something. He is keen to use players as part of state occasions and masques, elaborate and spectacular shows that celebrate the monarchy, far more frequently than Elizabeth ever did. He himself detests crowds but he recognises too that the people expect their King to put on a good show.

"James believes that Kings are appointed by God and their authority should not be questioned." Tom nodded. That seemed sensible enough. "But James is unusual."

"Because he's Scottish?"

"No. Well, yes that too. He reads, he thinks. He even writes. *The True Lawe of Free Monarchies* and a few other books, I believe." Tom was surprised but also impressed that someone who was King had time to write books. "He is something of a self-appointed expert."

"On what?"

"On whatever happens to be the topic of conversation. If he addresses you, Tom, mind your manners."

"That's hardly likely."

"That you have manners?"

"No, that he would deign to speak to me."

"He is the King, Tom. He does whatever he likes. Anyway, I have portrayed the witches as James describes them in another of his books, which he will be happy to discuss with anyone who is foolish enough to listen. *Demonologie* it is called. Full of bearded females with familiars, casting spells using foul ingredients to affect, amongst other things, the weather and cause a loss of sleep. He enjoys questioning those accused of witchcraft, mostly older women, and either pardoning them or sending them to Cambridge University for further examination."

Burbage entered and began delving through the rack at the back of the room, clearly looking for something.

"But, of course, he may not really believe all this."

"What do you mean?"

"Well, if there is an enemy, there must a conqueror. It allows him to draw powers to himself to be the saviour of the country. Politics and religion- it's a powerful combination."

"Hush, Will!" warned Burbage, selecting a dark cloak. "That is treasonous talk and could have us thrown in the Tower."

However, Cuthbert was able to use these shared interests to negotiate a rather interesting means of transport to get to where James wanted them to play: the Royal Palace at Hampton Court.

Chapter Fourteen
By Royal Command

'The play's the thing
Wherein I'll catch the conscience of the King.'
(*Hamlet*, II, (ii), l. 580)

Due to the amount of stage equipment and the lack of horses the company owned, James had agreed to allow them to use the Royal Barge, embarking from Richmond and arriving within a day at the riverside venue for the performance: Hampton Court.

Tom loved the trip on the water- he had only been briefly on a wherry once crossing the Thames and that was a matter of minutes. This was a wonderfully-leisurely journey, which offered a totally-unexpected view of the city where he had spent his entire life but which he now realised he hardly knew at all. They soon left the capital behind and looked out onto rolling fields and water-meadows. Carriages seemed to float along the shoreline and Tom felt a pang of envy for those whose life was so much easier than his. Then again, looking around at the faces on the barge, each full of anxious excitement, he wouldn't change places with anyone.

All too soon, on turning a bend in the river, Tom first glimpsed the riverside palace as they approached and his jaw just fell open.

"You'll catch flies in there," commented Heminges with a smile. Tom tried to regain his composure but it was difficult. He had never seen anything like it.

The palace that the barge was drawing towards was huge, made of distinctive red-brick and seemed like a castle from a child's story. The main building was an imposing structure and towers rose up from each corner. There were a few trees dotted around in front of the buildings but they failed to mask its sheer magnificence.

A courtier showed them the space where they were to perform-The Great Hall. As soon as they stepped into the space, Tom felt the air disappear from his lungs. Everywhere he looked, there was elaborately-carved woodwork, stained glass, tapestries depicting some Biblical scene which he only half-recognised and above all, light. There was what seemed like hundreds of candles and lamps that created an incredible glow. He had never set foot in a building anything like this and looking up, the roof seemed to go up forever.

Above where the temporary stage was being set up at one end, there was a giant window through which poured warm summer light, illuminating at that moment one of the huge tapestries that hung on the walls. He recognised, from his limited reading, the story of Abraham, prepared to obey God and sacrifice his own son if necessary.

Tom gulped. It felt a bit like he was being prepared to be sacrificed in this immense room that was more like a church than a place where a play might be performed. "But how can we stage the play here?" he stammered. "We will not be able to use trapdoors, smoke or wires."

"Very true, young Tom. Very true," agreed Will, marching into the room, much less in awe of the space. "There will also be no balcony to fall from and even less space for costume change."

"So how do we manage?"

"As we always do. We extemporise. Playhouse folk have to be amongst the quickest minds of all, Tom. A player falls sick, we must replace him. An effect doesn't work, we must find an alternative. A problem arises, we must solve it. But there is no need to panic. We have something that we can always come back to."

"And what is that?"

"The words. We must let the words work for us, Tom."

There was limited storage space but they had been careful in only bringing what they absolutely needed. There was a makeshift screen behind which all the costume changes had to take place and a door either side, creating a temporary tiring-house. Painted backdrops were used- castle battlements for the scenes in Macbeth's castle and wild landscape for the scenes outside.

There was a small so-called Minstrels' Gallery, a balcony where a small number of musicians might play but as with all other aspects of the production, it was a reduced version. None-the-less they had performed the play enough now to produce an effective show, without need for a prompt and without major mishap, apart from most recently, Edmund as a witch throwing all his ingredients into the cauldron in one go, making his later lines describing what he was putting into the pot, rather strange.

There were other differences compared to a 'normal' performance, like people actually looking after them. Will said the company spent three weeks at the Court the previous Christmas but this time, it would just be a couple of days. Still, even the most modest rooms were of such a level of luxury that Tom could not believe it. Crisp, white sheets, regular meals and each player had a daily allowance of a gallon and a half of ale. They were even treated by servants as guests! It was a different world and Tom absolutely loved it. The rest of the company went about their business as if nothing was out of the ordinary. They knew the place well but Tom walked around in a daze, his eyes standing out as if on stalks.

He had overcome several fears in recent months- he had spoken in front of others, stepped out upon the stage at The Globe and even fought for his life in a sword-fight. But there remained something else. He had been brought up to fear three things- God, his mother's wrath and the King. And he was about to meet one of them.

Tom wasn't even sure he'd recognise the King. After so many years of Elizabeth, many ordinary people had no idea what the King looked like. He'd only been on the throne for three years after all. Tom had only ever seen the King at a Royal procession a couple of years ago but that was some distance away. There was a rough image of the royal visage on the coins but the ones he saw were often worn almost smooth and even if they happened to have a shiny new penny, the likeness was not so wonderful that he felt confident that he would know the King in person.

However, on this occasion, he had some help in identifying the man in question. In the corridor outside The Great Hall, he paused in front of a giant portrait of James, positioned in a prime spot so that any visitor would have to pass by, making ownership of the palace and thereby of the crown, crystal clear.

Will came and stood beside him.

"What's he like?"

Will blew out his cheeks a bit like he had seen Edmund do and Tom wondered for a moment whether that was a family trait. "He is well-read, can speak French and Latin they say but…it's just that he holds an opinion on many things and will insist on telling you what it is until you share it. He's even written a book on poetry."

"He's written poems?"

"Well, not exactly. He's written a book about poems. And there's nothing he enjoys more than sharing his wisdom with people who actually write poems. Like me. So," he continued, "do not complain your life is hard." He softened his tone. "Perhaps we should not be too harsh on him."

"Why?"

"Well, imagine: since his birth, he's been surrounded by people who agree with him. I'm sure there have been times when you thought you knew everything." Tom's cheeks reddened and he remembered well enough being clipped round the ear by his mother. "Have no fear, Tom. He is a man. Just like any other."

But in this, Will was wrong. Not only was James, the largely-undisputed King of England and Scotland, not only was he known for his delight in tracking down witches and not only was he happy to share his opinion on any given subject until the point you agreed with him. He would soon be sitting in the same room as Tom and about to watch them perform a play. If what he saw displeased him, Tom and the others could swiftly find themselves in The Tower awaiting some deeply-unpleasant end. No, he was not like any other man.

In the afternoon, mid-way through a final rehearsal, a courtier approached and informed them that the King requested a private audience out in the gardens.

"Does the King know we are busy?" asked Will but the courtier just looked at him blankly. He turned to the rest of the company. "Alright, it seems now is a good time to have a break. Kings and small children," muttered Will as he and the courtier headed towards the entrance hall. "Neither understand the word 'No.'" Tom followed at a distance.

Will and James strolled around the elaborate gardens in the summer sunshine, Tom watching through a nearby window. James walked with his hands behind his back, looking very earnest and Will gave the impression of hanging on his every word.

Later, Cuthbert had a few last-minute orders.

"And one last thing. Under no account must anyone smoke a pipe around the King."

"Why not?"

"Because he hates the smell. Oh, by the way, do you have that list I gave you?"

"Yes," said Tom, wrinkling his nose. "I don't know where you expect me to get…things like that."

"Try the butcher's in the village. Not choice cuts- start with what he intends to throw away and make an offer as if you're doing him a favour. Do not speak of money unless he mentions it first and even then for goodness sake, haggle!"

An hour later, Tom passed the list to the man behind the counter who wordlessly, ran a grimy finger down the items, his frown deepening. "This wouldn't be for Will, by any chance?"

"Yes," indeed, confirmed Tom, astonished. "How did you know?"

The butcher gave a visible sigh of relief. "I'll see what I can do."

It was strange performing here as opposed to The Globe. They did not have to worry about the audience actually attending and when they did, they were all seated and although not completely silent, they were certainly much better behaved than the drunken rabble in the yard.

The smaller space and the fact that the stage was enclosed by walls and of course, a roof made the sound travel better in some ways but there was also an echo which meant they had to slow their delivery.

The audience were mostly in front of the players too so they had to be a little more careful about turning away from them. Since this was a Royal performance, Will had impressed upon them all the importance of directing their main attention towards where James was sitting. As long as he could see and hear everything, the rest of the audience were mostly unimportant.

There was tiered seating to the left and right in front of the players and in the middle would sit the most important person of all- the King with any family or special guests who were being honoured. The standard platform or dais was still not high enough for the King who would occupy a level still higher- there was strictly no-one who had a higher seat or better view than the King. James liked Oriental carpets that were laid over his special part of the platform and he would sit on a throne-like 'elbow chair,' generously covered with delicately-embroidered cushions.

The remainder of the floor of the hall and stage itself was covered with green cloth and servants had busily strewn flowers about the hall to disperse any offensive odours. There was a fireplace but it remained unlit as it was not needed on such a warm summer evening.

The platform and the canopy were known as 'State'. Your status was shown by how close to the stage you were and how close to this royal platform. Seating was not allocated and there was always a great crush to secure the most prestigious seats. Reputations could be enhanced or royal disfavour shown if a place was gained particularly close or far away from the most important positions. Several officers, armed with rods, had the unenviable task of getting the spectators into some kind of order and at times they would have to set about the heads of those invited to deal with disputes, like a shepherd herding an unruly bunch of sheep.

The day drew late and the hour drew late. Even if the performance fee was modest, the company had a generous meal, which was good except Heminges always wanted to over-eat and then with an excess of ale, he would fall asleep and miss his cue. Once, back at The Globe, his snoring from the tiring-house could even be clearly heard amongst the audience and Condell had to go and kick him awake.

Eventually, the banquet was over and whispers went around that the King would soon arrive and Tom pressed up against the extemporised traverse. He had never seen a King, not a real one. Not like this. Not until now.

A hush fell across the room and two trumpeters entered the far end of the hall, took up position either side of the door and blasted a fanfare that made Tom jump. Everyone stood and waited. Moments later, several courtiers entered and in their midst a man who seemed to be dressed in thick clothes as if for winter. He strode confidently into the hall, waving to his invited guests who returned the gesture with bows and curtseys. He took up his prime position on the dais and only when he sat, did the audience resume their seats. He seemed slightly awkward and Tom remembered what other players had said about James not liking crowds and preferring smaller gatherings of people.

Sometimes when he was nervous, Tom set himself some kind of mental problem, to distract himself. While the audience were settling themselves and final preparations were being made to start the performance, he gazed through the traverse at the most important man in England and tried to work out his age. Ned had said he was born in 1587. That made him…39. Almost as old as Will. But the two men looked very different.

James was thinner than Will but sported a similar beard of formal cut, although his hair was quite a strong ginger colour. Now that Tom was involved in creating and maintaining costume, he took a slightly more critical eye of clothing. James was quite a dishevelled mess. There were jewels, there was a lace collar and there was a fur wrapped around his shoulder- all high quality but none of the items really complemented each other. He was quite tall and even given the robes that he was wearing, Tom could see his shoulders were fairly broad. His legs however stuck out strangely from his doublet like those of a gangly bird.

The audience fell quiet and the performance began. Will had impressed upon the cast the need to be serious in their performance so there was less spontaneous clowning, tumbling or comic business.

James himself was an odd-looking fellow. His tongue lolled out of his mouth when he spoke and he was forever fidgeting with his codpiece, even in public. Despite the fact that he was always attended by several burly bodyguards who looked like they would take great pleasure in running anyone through with a sword, James himself insisted on wearing several layers of bulky clothing in case a murderer tried to stab him. He seemed like an awkward squirming schoolboy but Will had impressed upon them the importance of not underestimating James.

He even said that James was overseeing a new version of the Bible, which, according to Will, might even be an improvement upon the original. Tom found it hard to understand how anyone could rewrite the Bible. To him, that was like saying someone was going to repaint the sky.

As they were indoors, light was provided by a large number of candles, which provided suitable atmosphere, especially in the night scenes and the tense exchanges between Macbeth and his wife. However, it did mean that the candles had to be replaced and so rather unusually, there was a short break in the play, during which Armin, still in character as the Porter, announced that they may eat and drink something to pass the time. It worked well but Tom could see he would have to plan for such a thing in the future.

The King called for some wine, which he proceeded to slurp like a thirsty puppy, spilling some and licking his lips afterwards with his strangely-long tongue. Those in his immediate circle were used to this and paid him no attention but those seeing him for the first time stared a little at their King whose table manners seemed to leave quite a lot to be desired. Tom had heard a Scottish accent before but found James' hard to follow and now understood why Will had not attempted to perform the entire play in that way.

During one of the witches' scenes, Tom became aware of a really unpleasant smell drifting across the stage.

"Why did you use the sulphur?" he hissed at one of the apprentices. He had been quite clear in his instructions about what effects could be used in such a small space, especially with such an important guest present. What would he be thinking?

"I didn't," the boy protested.

"Well, what on earth is that smell then?" The boy nervously pointed.

Tom followed his finger in disbelief. The source of the stench was none other than…James himself. People said he only took a bath little more than once a year and from the odours around the stage, Tom could believe it.

At this moment, something else became clear. He had been puzzled by his errand to the butcher's but gave a nod of understanding when the witches started dropping a number of choice items, including supposedly 'Eye of newt and toe of frog, wool of bat and tongue of dog,' into their cauldron making the audience recoil in disgust. James however roared with laughter. His tastes were a little more coarse that that of Elizabeth who always favoured the comedies.

The Porter scene also provoked a strong reaction. Will had written a piece for Armin to show his comic ability as a servant woken up in the middle of the night and taking a long time to open the gate to Macbeth's castle. The idea was that since the King had been murdered there, the Porter was the now the gatekeeper to Hell but that wasn't really what James was interested in. The moment where Armin found time to relieve himself while talking about the effects of drink on the human body had the King howling with laughter.

When the play came to an end, there was a collective holding of breath as James slowly rose to his feet, the audience following his movements as much as the players for some sign of a reaction. Time seemed to stand still but he eventually began to clap, slowly at first but with greater enthusiasm, joined in by the audience, more from a sense of relief than genuine pleasure. He leaped forward to shake the hand of each of the players but saved his warmest congratulations for Burbage in the title role and for Will as the creative force behind it all.

"Another fine performance, Mr Shakespeare."

"As ever, your servant," replied Will with a deep bow.

"And yet, you performed for Essex." Tom remembered what Burbage had said about this infamous traitor.

"We are but humble players, your Highness. We performed the play because we were paid to do so. We were offered 40 shillings extra."

"Your 30 pieces of silver, eh? He purposely asked for *Richard II*, knowing full well that it contained the removal of a King. You are the mirror of the time. Three thousand come to your playhouse theatre daily. Yes, I have my sources. If you want to start a revolt, a playhouse would be a good place to start."

"Perhaps, your Highness. But as you so rightly observe, that is only if you wish to start a revolt. Which we do not."

James gave Will a long stare. He was never entirely sure with these temperamental, artistic types. "So business is good?"

"Well, not exactly. As I am sure your Highness has heard, we have been forced to close due to plague."

"Ah, yes. Nasty business."

"And we lost a great deal of revenue due to similar events last autumn."

"Our offices were otherwise engaged. It was the time of those evil plotters who would destroy the fabric of our state."

"We were not here in the city during the plot."

"Ah, yes. That's very…convenient."

"No, your Highness. It was not. It was very far from convenient. We had to go on tour."

"Ah, yes," repeated James, as if details had just floated into his mind by accident and were not always there. "Oxford, I seem to remember amongst other places."

"That's right. You seem very well informed."

"We have…our sources. It is sensible to keep everyone in view. Even such…loyal subjects as yourself."

James was never entirely sure how far Will could be trusted. He had shown no interest in becoming involved in Royal masques, which were increasingly fashionable and spectacular celebrations of the Monarchy and which would have been financially lucrative. Perhaps he liked to think of himself as a free-thinking artist or perhaps he could integrate such elements within his existing plays. There was some Catholicism in the background of parts of Will's family too and he had shown himself to be a man who knew his own mind as well as a writer of considerable promise. Perhaps, thought James, it was better to keep a potentially-dangerous dog on a leash, albeit a long one.

Suddenly James started to shriek madly, pointing at a nearby gentlewoman in the audience. The guards reacted swiftly, throwing themselves heroically in front of the Monarch, blocking the course of any weapon aimed at killing the King. In moments, the woman was wrestled to the ground, searched and found to be in possession of a suspicious object- the reason for the king's consternation.

"There!" cried James. "A familiar!" All eyes turned to the object, which the woman did seem reluctant to let go but was persuaded to do so after several rapiers were held to her throat.

"Bring it here," commanded the King, drawing his own sword. The object was set before him and he prodded it suspiciously, eventually skewering it and lifting it up to the light of the nearest candle.

"As I suspected," he declared. "A toad!" He glared back at the woman still pinned in her seat by armed guards. "Explain yourself, witch. Why have you sent one of your familiars against me?"

"I am no witch," the woman cried hotly. "And that is no familiar." Some people believed that witches used animals, or so-called 'familiars,' to spy on others and report back to them. James was one such person.

"Kindly explain what it is then?" demanded James, twirling his punctured victim with some relish.

"Bring it to me and I will show you."

James paused. "Alright. But no tricks. Guards, be alert."

He stepped over to the woman who sat up gingerly. As James approached, stretching out his arm, she reached up and took the green object carefully from the blade. "It is no familiar," she repeated. "See." She carefully and slowly opened it, mindful of the rather nervous guards around her. "It is a purse."

"A what?"

"A purse. Look, there is my money." She held up a few coins, almost apologetically. "There is no danger."

James squinted at her suspiciously. "Why do you carry a purse shaped like a toad?"

"It is not a toad. It is a frog. I bought it in the market hereabouts. They are the latest fashion- purses made to look like animals or fruit or I don't know what."

James looked at her with some disgust. "We must keep our wits about us when there is such idolatry. Guards, return to your positions. Madam, I apologise but I urge you to reconsider your choice of design. This evening might have had a tragic outcome."

Every single member of the audience was each sworn to secrecy on pain of death. James did not want gossip spread about such incidents. He was aware that the general opinion of him was still mixed and yet, neither could he just ignore his convictions about the witchcraft which he saw at work all around him.

Tom looked concerned. "Is James not worried that someone will talk?" he whispered to Will.

Will's expression darkened like a cloud passing in front of the sun. "Did you not hear what he said?" He drew a line with his forefinger under his neck. "'On pain of death' means exactly that. Besides, history is written by the rich and powerful. Twas ever thus."

Chapter Fifteen

On Tour

'To thine own self be true.'
(*Hamlet*, I, (iii), l. 78)

They toured through September until the leaves began to fall from the trees. Tom had told his mother that he was helping with harvesting and needed to stay on a farm some distance away. He didn't like the thought of leaving her alone but what else could he do? He couldn't stay and beg on plague-ridden streets. With the money he would hopefully earn on tour, they had a chance of not starving.

The contrast in his fortunes could not be greater. One night, sleeping in Hampton Court Palace; a few days later, camping out in a ditch. To tour as a travelling player was like a step back in time to a way of life before the playhouses were built. It was hard, packing up the barest essentials and travelling sometimes long distances to places where they might not receive a warm welcome.

Once outside London, they were viewed as purveyors of plague or dubious morality and often forbidden to enter settlements. It depended very much how well they were received by the Mayor or Chief Bailiff. If there was some trust there, perhaps a relationship with the company's patron, then they might perform but often the Mayor would just send them away. Will's reputation, his great works- it all counted for nothing.

If they were given permission to enter a town, the musicians and dancers in the company would make the most of this and form a procession, producing as much noise as possible to make everyone aware they had arrived. This would always be led by Armin, turning somersaults and seeking to charm the people. Sometimes it worked.

Financially, it was a lean time. Many of the company could not be taken on tour so found themselves without a job even before the tour began. The hit-and-miss nature of the welcome made a regular income difficult. The size of any potential audience was much smaller than in London and made up of fewer wealthy citizens.

In terms of where they performed, they set up a temporary stage in town squares, on village greens and sometimes if they were lucky, in the halls of manor houses or the yards of inns where some rudimentary lighting was possible. By The Globe's standards, attendance was poor. This later situation was often especially difficult as the audience was frequently drunk and more liable to shout out during performances. For the older members of the company, this was nothing new but for Tom it was a challenge.

As they entered the outskirts of a small town near Oxford, they passed a parish church, outside which a couple of beggars were sitting, seeking alms. Tom always felt bad walking past beggars. He was one himself after all but if he stopped to help one, others would expect donations too. And to be honest, he didn't have the money to help even one.

Still, he did what he usually did, which was to look directly in the eye of those poor unfortunate souls and smile. He knew from his own begging experience, that they would feel a sense of disappointment, hopelessness and probably anger too but it was still better at the end of a day to remember the boy who smiled at you than a scowling face or even worse, just to be ignored.

They stopped to pitch camp on a small field outside the village. Edmund managed to stumble into them, half-asleep. "What hour is it?"

Will looked up at the sky. "Light thickens and the crow makes wing to the rooky wood."

"Huh?"

"It is nearly twilight."

"Right." Edmund wandered off.

Tom chuckled as he had recognised the lines from *Macbeth*. "You see, Tom, life sometimes needs a bit of a helping hand to allow us to see the poetry around us."

The following day, once they had set up a temporary stage on the village green and done their best to attract some attention, they spent the time before an afternoon performance sitting on the ground, sharing a modest lunch of dry bread and a little cheese. The contrast with their previous fortunes could not have been greater.

Cuthbert passed by, doing a good impression of someone who had used up all available patience. Will asked him what was amiss.

"Sorry Will, I know he's your brother but we just can't do anything with him."

"Put him in charge of…I don't know, possets."

"Possets?"

"You know- the drinks Lady Macbeth uses to drug the King's guards."

Later, just before the performance was due to start, Cuthbert was frantically looking behind the temporary stage for some important props. "Where are the possets?"

"What possets?" answered Edmund, his speech a little slurred.

"That's my question, you dullard! We need there to be something on stage so that those poor players have something to hold- now where are they?"

"Oh, right." Edmund grinned.

Cuthbert paused and took in Edmund's vacant expression at a glance. "Have you been drinking?" There were heavy fines for drinking while 'on duty'. It didn't bother Tom but he knew some of the older players struggled to avoid a crafty pint of wine before a show.

"Maybe a little. I had to test them."

"Test what?"

"The possets. If they're strong enough to knock out the guards, they need to be quite strong."

There was a pause. Cuthbert spoke slowly but clearly, a sign with which Tom was now familiar of rising anger. "Am I to understand, you made real possets and then tested them. By drinking both of them?" Edmund nodded. "Listen, you…dolt. The possets do not have to be real. There does not even have to be liquid in the cups. It is a play. These are players. They can pretend. Understand? Pretend. Just like you can pretend to be a human being."

Edmund kept on nodding but soon enough the effect of the possets took hold and he slumped in a corner, snoring deeply.

The company performed to a small crowd and while they were appreciative, the number of coins that Condell had managed to collect in a small bag didn't make much of a 'chink' as he shook it.

Afterwards, Heminges, usually needing little encouragement to drink, suggested they try a local inn. Having found one, talk turned to money, never far from their thoughts.

"Are we rich then, Will?" asked Tom. The ale flowed much more slowly and the mood was much more subdued than the last time they were in a tavern.

"Our performance for the King will yield a fee but not a large one. Probably no more than ten pounds." Tom's eyes had lit up. "Yes, well it may sound a lot but there is so much expense in running a playhouse, it will not go far. James is very careful about money. It is the source of many arguments with Parliament. Of more value to us, is the protection of his approval."

Tom wasn't in charge of the finances of the company of course- that was mainly Burbage's area of expertise- but he was a little worried. He didn't want the company to be declared bankrupt and have to return to a life on the streets.

Will caught some of this from his thoughtful expression. "What says our rising star? Worry not, Tom. All the money in Christendom will not make you happy. Business is how we live but Art…Art, Tom is *why* we live."

Tom wasn't sure. A few extra pennies might be nice. Some decent food and clothes. The chance to buy things for his mother. Some better flowers for his father's grave. He couldn't pay for those with 'Art'.

"Is there not some small part of you that secretly wishes to be rich,

Will?" asked Heminges, taking a deep swig from a tankard. "You are scarcely a beggar these days."

Tom knew that Will was a shareholder in the company, and that he'd got property and other investments up in Stratford. Ned had even told him that after rebuilding New Place, his big house up there, he even sold the leftover stone back to the council. He was certainly no fool.

Will shrugged. "I have some measure of fame, friends, and some substantial property. More I must not look to have. The bubble reputation means little to me." Tom was about to agree that it meant little to him as well but then realised that Will wasn't making a joke.

"Besides," said Will, turning morose for a moment, "to whom can I pass my good fortune? I have no son. Not now. My wife will have no further issue and my daughters remain unmarried. Perhaps they will marry but perhaps not. Without a male heir, my status as a gentleman will die with me."

"What about the scribblers?" asked Condell, putting his rapier aside at the end of a practice session. He had worked hard with the wrestling in *As You like It* and was now working out the fights between Macbeth, played by Burbage and his various rivals. Tom was in attendance, a script in his hand as usual. Although a man of action, Condell also cared about the words the players spoke. Often, rival companies planted scribes in the crowd to copy the play as it was performed.

Will however seemed unconcerned. "What they take away is usually a fairly poor version of the original."

Condell was surprised at his cool reaction. "But does that not annoy you? They are stealing your words."

Will dismissed this with a wave of his hand. "We should be flattered at the idea our work is so desirable. Besides, the words do not belong to me. As you have all noted, many of my plays are peppered with new words of my own invention. It is one way I can make such practices ineffective. If they do not know what the words mean, it will be at least frustrating for them and maybe even impossible to perform the piece."

Condell chuckled. He had never thought of it like that. "You sir, are a genius."

Will shook his head. "You are clothing me in borrowed robes. Arthur Brooke wrote *Romeo and Juliet*. Thomas Lodge wrote *Rosalynde*, which I use in *As You Like It*. *A Comedy of Errors* is very like Plautus. The story of *King Lear* is not of my invention. The two parts of *Henry the Fourth*, *Henry the Fifth*, *Richard the Third*- I could go on. All of these stories existed already. I am the real thief."

"YOU ARE NOT!" Tom shocked himself by his own hot temper, animated a little by the ale, which he did not usually drink so freely. "You are worth more than all of the others."

Will smiled. "I thank you for you kind words, albeit a little jarring on the ear. Plot, dialogue, titles- what do they matter? When someone tells a story or a joke, do you really think no-one has told that before? Do you say, 'Cease fellow, unless this is a true and original jest, written by your own hand?'" Reluctantly, Tom shook his head. "The art is in the telling.

Remember, *Romeo and Juliet* opens with a sonnet telling everyone with ears to hear what happens and how the play will end. Has that made it any less popular?" Tom, still relatively-new to the company wasn't sure how to answer. "No- it remains a firm favourite to this day. When crowds flock to see a tragedy, they know the hero will die. They expect, even demand, it. It's not what happens but how it happens that matters.

"Ideas do not belong to me. They are for everyone. You only copy what you do not fully understand. Besides, it is many times better than being ignored. And anyway, frustration is the very nature of humanity. A life without struggle is no life at all."

Tom joined in. "That's not quite what Heminges meant. I think" He tried to express his thoughts but they were like the slippery fish they landed down by the river every morning. The harder he tried to grab them, the more they slipped from his grasp. "Don't you wish...don't you wish there was a way to...keep these words somehow?"

"I'm not sure I follow you."

"Well, you write a play, people see it and then you must write a whole new one. What happens to your work?"

"It lives on. In here," he said, tapping his forehead "and more importantly," pointing to his heart, "in here. That's more eternal than a thousand heavens to me."

"But what about a record of your work?"

"The play's the thing. A great cook does not keep a dish for years afterwards but carefully crafts ingredients for the pleasure of a time spent with friends and the memory of that time to be revisited perhaps in old age. Your…books are like a maggotty pie.

"Besides, can you imagine rows of schoolboys being forced to read my plays? In fact, anyone reading my plays. What would be the point of that?" They all laughed at the absurdity of the idea.

Will's tone turned a little more serious. "What will live beyond you, Tom?"

He thought for a moment, a tendency that Will had come to appreciate in the boy. "Everything, I suppose. People younger than me. The sun will still rise and set."

"A sound answer. But that is not what I meant. I mean, what will survive of *you*."

"Me?"

"Yes, what will record that you ever existed?"

Tom thought for a moment. The conversation had taken a rather dark tone. "A gravestone, I suppose. I don't know where." He hadn't given any thought to such matters but the fact was that people of his standing in the world often ended up in a pauper's grave with little to mark the spot as he knew all too well.

"Another sound answer. But consider this, 50 years from now, everyone who ever knew you will be dead."

"But-"

"-Alright, maybe 60. 70, if you must but you see the idea? At some point, your existence in the memory of others will be lost."

"Why are you telling me this?"

"There will be no statues and paintings for people to marvel at my face. It doesn't matter, Tom. I shall be dust."

"It doesn't matter!" The words burst out of him, scaring himself a little and even Will took a step back. "It DOES matter. These plays, these words are yours."

But Will was shaking his head. "No, Tom. You're wrong. These words don't belong to me. I'm only borrowing them for a while. They belong to everyone. If we allow only priests and noblemen to read, then they will be the ones who control us. Words and ideas are for everyone. And without words, there can be no ideas."

"BEHOLD!" They all instinctively turned at such a loud interruption. "Pray, let us worship at the altar of the great William Shakespeare."

"Edmund," began, Will. "Come and sit down. You're drunk."

For some strange reason, nothing infuriated Edmund more than people telling him he was drunk. Even when he was. He had tried to be a player, he really had but whatever he did, he just seemed to spoil things. Everyone knew it, including unfortunately himself.

"Of course, dear brother," he replied in a tone which suggested Will was far from 'dear.' "You are no better than a lap-dog, doing the King's bidding, even wearing the livery of the king, performing in his palaces."

"You are right," agreed Will, taking some of the venom from his adversary's expression. "The playhouse, which I partly own, is filled every day. I have managed what my father could not. We have a family coat of arms- with a falcon and a spear, no less. And our Latin motto, 'Non sanz droict,' Not Without Right," he added, translating helpfully, "shows that we have deserved such things. Some may say they are mere trinkets but such is life. Money and status are easy to spurn when you do not have them."

Will's words were like a spider's web spun around Edmund's mind who did not have the firepower to reply. He opted for more direct insults. "You have forgotten where you come from."

This managed to nettle Will who grabbed the front of his jacket and pulled him very close. "I will never forget that. It is who I am." He released his grip and pushed him away. "The independence of which you speak is nothing more than a dream. I have no wish to become a poor boy from Warwickshire again."

"But at least you would follow your own advice. What is that line from Polonius in *Hamlet*? 'To thine own self be true.'"

"Sit down, Edmund," suggested Burbage and put out an arm to steady the younger man who was unsteady on his feet.

"I can take my ale," shouted Edmund, angrily shaking him off. "I'm not a drunk." He turned and promptly walked into one of the low beams in the tavern, stunning himself for a moment. "Come on, William. Dispute this like a man."

"I'm not going to fight you."

"Why? Are you scared?"

"No. I have no wish to fight you." Marlowe had been in his mind recently.

"I think you're a coward…a lil-, lill-, lilly-livered coward." He finally managed the word. Slowly, he drew a dagger from inside his tunic. The others around Will backed off.

"Calm down, Edmund, there's a good fellow."

He whirled round at Burbage. "DON'T TALK TO ME LIKE A BOY!" he roared. "I am a Shakespeare. I am born of a great family. I-I-" He ran out of boasts.

"Sit down, Edmund," said Will calmly.

"I am not a schoolboy."

"More's the pity. You might have learned something."

"Are you going to fight?" Edmund brought the dagger right up to William's cheek. His hand was far from steady from all the ale he had drunk and the others looked on in some fear.

Only Will remained calm. "Are you going to put that down?"

Edmund managed a dismissive laugh and he brought his drunken face right next to Will's. "Make me."

Will sighed as if he was faced with the most tiresome situation. But then suddenly in a blur of movement, he grabbed hold of Edmund's arm, the one carrying the knife and twisted it sharply. Edmund cried out, dropped the knife instantly and with a roar of anger and pain, lunged at Will who met this charge with a straight fist.

Without time even to grunt, Edmund was knocked out cold and landed with a thud on the tavern paving stones.

There was a silence.

Will sighed again. "Condell, take him out to the stables and tie him up with the horses."

"Is that wise?"

"The horses won't mind." He looked at them all. "I know what you mean. He'll sleep it off."

He looked down at his brother, who was now snoring loudly as

Condell, helped by several apprentices, carried him out. "You know the worst thing about Edmund?" Burbage, Heminges and Tom looked at each other, hardly knowing where to start. "He reminds me of myself at his age: ambitious, angry, frustrated. We must try and save him. I am determined that he should not go the way of Kempe."

"Who?" asked Tom.

"William Kempe," explained Heminges. "Our resident clown before Armin took on that role."

"What happened to him?"

Will took up the story. "Kempe was a great player, truly gifted but…" For once, words seemed to fail him.

"But what?"

He still paused as if what he was about to say was painful. "No-one is greater than the company. We all have our jobs to do and we do them well but he, well, he started to extemporise lines."

"You mean when he forgot them?"

"No, although that can be bad enough sometimes. No, I mean he took it upon himself to improve upon those lines written for him."

"Ah."

"And his clowning threatened to overwhelm whole plays. And then there was his jig."

"The dance he did at the end?"

"Yes," said Will, coldly, clearly not impressed. "I understand that it's good to send the crowd away happy but he would be like a small child dancing for his favourite uncle. The thing would go on and on. You know how some groundlings can be quite drunk by the end too. Well, it all came to a head and he refused to reduce his antics and so…we agreed that he should leave the company.

"It was a difficult decision and unfortunately, it didn't end well for him. The applause soon died when it was just his one-man-show on offer." Will wandered over to the bar to negotiate another round of drinks.

"You know," said Burbage, leaning forward. "Kempe danced all the way from London to Norwich in nine days."

Tom did not look impressed but that was mainly because he had no idea where Norwich was.

"It's north of here," explained Burbage. "About 100 miles."

"But what's wrong with Edmund?" asked Tom, expressing what was really on his mind.

The company's elder statesman looked at Tom. "Do you still not understand?" Tom's expression suggested he did not. "He's jealous."

"Of who?"

"Well, you mostly." Tom stared, dumbstruck. "Of course. You are everything he wishes he was. Honest, hard-working, clever. To see you, reminds him of everything he is not. You are Will's favourite now."

"But-"

"-You know it's so." Tom fell silent. There was nothing he could do. He hadn't sought out Will's praise or patronage but it was true that Will now looked upon him almost as a son, his only son.

Several hours later, Tom was dispatched to check on Edmund who had come round and was already regretting his impulsive action, not least because he had found his brother to possess a better punch than he expected.

"Where did he learn to fight like that?" His nose was still clogged with blood and it made his voice come out funny.

"I have no idea," answered Tom honestly. "Maybe he was a soldier for a while. There's quite a lot about fighting in his plays, you know."

"Will?" Edmund tried to laugh and the idea but he just winced in pain.

"Edmund, you must...calm yourself." Tom shook his head. "Why are you always so...angry?"

Edmund blew out his cheeks in frustration, trying to clear the fuzziness in his head. "It's hard to explain." He paused to try and gather his thoughts. "I was never enough for my father. Will was always away in London, doing great things. The only reports we heard of him were all glowing. My reports...well, let's say, I wasn't exactly a genius at school and it's hard for anyone to see what little light you produce if you're standing next to the sun.

Just imagine, Tom, everywhere you go, as soon as you say your name, people look at you differently. First there's curiosity. Am I the famous Will Shakespeare? They look me up and down but clearly I don't match their expectations. Then I say, I am his younger brother and they are disappointed but still a little curious. Do I write too? they ask. No, I reply and the curiosity vanishes.

"Then imagine growing up in a small town where everyone knows your name but not from anything *you*'ve done. Ever since I was born, there have been almost daily reports of my elder brother's exploits and successes. And what I achieved? I cannot find a woman who will marry me. I cannot keep regular employment. I cannot even leave Stratford without my brother's help."

"Are you not proud of Will's achievements?"

"Of course but it is like I'm a ghost. At least when I get into fights, people can see me."

At that very moment, Burbage was bringing matters to a head in the tavern. "Will, we have to do something about Edmund. Either he will die in a pub brawl or at the end of a rope."

A silence settled on the group as they wrestled with this thorny problem. "I have an idea," said a voice eventually. All eyes slowly turned to Heminges. "After years of negotiating with the Master of the Revels, I still have a few friends who owe me a favour or two."

A couple of days later, the company was rehearsing on another village green, when Edmund suddenly appeared, dressed in a costume that Will did not remember seeing before.

"What do you think?" A sober Edmund put his arms out and twirled round to display a dark blue uniform.

"Very…impressive. Is this for our next production?" He frowned at Heminges. Since Ned's death, they had all had to pitch in and help with costumes.

"No. I'm done with that. I talked to Heminges here-" the older man stood behind him, beaming.

"-and he told me about a vacancy for a Constable that had arisen in Cheapside and if I was agreeable, he could put my name forward and amazingly, of all the applicants, they wanted me."

"Amazing," echoed Will, meeting Heminges gaze with a silent but knowing look.

Constables were not renowned for their brainpower and patrolled the city, especially after dark, looking for troublemakers. They had few powers and were largely seen as figures of fun but Edmund seemed pleased with his new status.

"I get my own uniform, get to patrol the streets, get some respect and you know what's best of all?"

"You get to test ale?"

"No- well, yes, there is that too. No, it's even better than that. I get to break up fights!" He turned to Will. "I wanted to thank you, brother."

"For making your life miserable?"

"No. For giving me a chance. The life of a player is not for everyone. I know that now." He went around the entire company, showing off his new uniform.

"Be careful, Edmund," warned Armin. "If you fall asleep on duty or find yourself hanging around without much to do, you might have to arrest yourself for vagrancy."

Edmund smiled but with a slight frown as he suddenly wondered if that was actually true.

"Somehow the streets seem less safe that they were before," murmured Armin to Tom. "A cheap fellow for Cheapside. A real Dogberry." Tom looked at him in incomprehension. "Dogberry's a hopeless Constable in *Much Ado About Nothing*." That was a play Tom had yet to read. "Always falling asleep and getting mixed up."

"Ah, yes," said Tom. "A real Dogberry."

"Was there really a vacancy?" Will asked Heminges under his breath.

"In a way," the older man conceded, patting his large belly. "Quite a number have just died from the plague." Will went a little pale.

Chapter Sixteen

A Ghost from the Past

'A great reckoning in a little room.'
(*As You Like It*, III, (iii), l. 11)

The worst of the plague was over and the company had returned to The Globe. It was the last day of *Macbeth*. Will was already working on his version of *King Lear* and there would be the usual mad rush to get a production ready. Tom was still concentrating on Lady Macbeth and trying to get her transformation right. She had few scenes but she was different in each one. Her madness and death had to seem believable from what the crowd had seen up to that point.

They were about twenty minutes in and Macbeth had met the witches, been tempted by their prophecy and now Tom was about to make his entrance as Lady Macbeth, reading a letter recounting events in the story so far but also showing how close husband and wife were and how she could only hope for any improvement in her own life through his success.

He stepped out, letter in hand and walked slowly to the centre of the stage, about to deliver his opening line, when a couple of apple-cores whizzed past his head. He instinctively scanned the crowd for the source of the missiles and felt a sudden, sharp pain in the pit of his stomach as if he'd just been stabbed. Front and centre in the yard was a face he recognised. A face he used to have nightmares about. A face that had come to represent everything he used to hate about himself. It was Jack.

He'd almost forgotten about his past but it seemed his past had not forgotten about him. Looking back, it was ridiculous to think he was somehow miraculously safe there in The Globe. Just because he felt that way, did not mean he was protected by some sort of magic. Every day he saw folk walk in off the street and as long as they had a penny, they could enter.

And what was worse, Jack was leering right at him, seeing past the wig, the make-up, the dress, past all that to the scared little boy whom he used to bully. A thin smile crept across his features. Normally, he was accompanied by a few of the gang, there to laugh at his jokes and do what he said but today he didn't think he'd need them. To pay a penny represented a few missed meals but he thought it was worth it if it meant the opportunity to make Tom wriggle like a worm on a hook.

Tom took his place onstage and tried to carry on but was clearly distracted and stumbled over his first line. At this point in the scene he was alone onstage and in the tiring-house Burbage was clearly aware that something was amiss but not sure what. A few in the yard laughed and Jack looked around with all the relish of a fox before a defenceless chicken.

"Well, well, if it isn't me old friend, Tom Swann." Jack's voice cut through the crowd who fell silent, unsure of exactly what was happening. "Yes, ladies and gentlemen," continued Jack, used to taking command and attention. "We're looking at a little boy, a very unconvincing boy, a scared little boy…in a dress." There was some laughter at this but most audience members turned to the newcomer. They were used to the idea of female parts being played by boys and it wasn't really anything out of the ordinary. Sometimes comments from the yard provided better entertainment than what was on offer on stage. As yet, they were undecided.

"Come on, Tom. Cat got ya tongue? Show yourself. As you really are."

By now, there was a complete stillness in the yard. The crowd still didn't know why the groundling was doing this and it clearly was not part of the play but it felt like something was coming to a head. A challenge had been laid down.

Slowly, Tom walked to the centre of the stage. He could hear his own breathing and he was sure the crowd could hear his heartbeat too, thudding through his layers of clothing. Several moments passed and he still did not speak. Burbage and Will exchanged anxious glances.

Then something happened that no-one seemed to have expected. Tom stretched out a hand to Jack as if he was asking him to dance. Jack looked about him, perplexed. Tom's open palm made a beckoning gesture.

Jack snorted to himself. If the little fool really wanted to be humiliated further, why deny the crowd their fun? He strolled forward, waving at the crowd, who started to applaud and whistle. At the edge of the stage, he looked around for some means to climb up as it was as high as his nose but several sturdy fellows reacted spontaneously, came forward and heaved him up.

"Right, then," said Jack, brushing himself down and starting to preen himself like a cockerel. Now that he was the focus of attention, his chest swelled out and he adopted a swagger in stepping towards Tom. "Perhaps we can see the real boy beneath the dress." Tom held his gaze for just a second and then, still without a word, drew his dress to one side, revealing the petticoat beneath.

There were wolf-whistles from the crowd in anticipation at the sight of a bit of flesh. Jack's smile had faded a little as Tom's reaction was not quite what he'd expected.

Tom for his part, still with the demure actions of a lady, reached beneath his petticoats and after several moments, drew out a rapier and before Jack could react, held it up to his rival's throat.

"No, Tom-" began Burbage and took a step forward but Will hissed at him to be still.

"Ah, now, Tom," said Jack, backing off slightly. "'Twas only a bit of fun. Er, you know, how we like to joke." He gave a nervous laugh and looked round but the crowd were silent now and no-one was coming to his aid. He took a second small step back, the blade still held to his throat, making him rise up on tip-toes. The swagger and the smile had gone.

"I'm sure we can talk about this," he babbled. "Man-to-er, well, you understand." Another step back. He was right at the edge of the stage now. He glanced back, aware of the drop. Another step and he'd-

Slowly, Tom lowered his sword a fraction and Jack relaxed a little, his grin returning but more from nervous relief than confidence now.

Tom, still adopting the manner of a lady rather than a 13-year-old boy, tilted his head slightly and with the sword, flipped open Jack's tunic, as if looking for something.

Jack looked down, bemused himself. "No money in there." He half turned to the crowd, aware that he'd had his back to them, like a poor player. "What d'you fink I am? Some kind of cutpurse?"

With a deft flick of his wrist, Tom exposed a couple of secret pockets in Jack's tunic, specifically-made to hide something. He cut through a few key threads and several purses fell out upon the stage with a thud. There was a gasp from the crowd.

Tom stepped forward and carefully scooped one up. He held it out to the crowd like a prize kill in a hunt. There was an 'Ooooh' from the groundlings who had clearly heard Jack's protestations of innocence.

"I....I....I found it," stammered Jack with the standard defence of a thief. The crowd almost laughed at his cheek. Thieves were often tied to the pillory post nearby and pelted with rotten fruit.

Tom paraded the item at the front of the stage. Although it was small, it was also distinctive. Moleskin with a decorative 'P' sewn into it. He did not speak but his meaning was clear. If the owner of the purse was present, they should make themselves known.

There was a muffled cry from one of the galleries and the sound of marching feet. Soon a figure pushed through the groundlings, his progress visible by an ostrich feather that seemed to be making its own way towards the stage.

Finally, feather, hat and the person upon whom it stood were all visible. "It is mine," said the man, used to commanding and sounding distinctly unhappy. "I am the First Earl of Pembroke. I demand that you return my property."

"Of course," replied Tom, quietly that only those very close to him could hear. "Without extemporisation." The man's eyes widened as he realised to whom he was speaking. Tom lowered the sword and allowed the nobleman to retrieve his purse and swiftly returned to his place.

Tom turned his attention back to the thief. The mood in the crowd had shifted slightly and Tom could feel a growing sense of anger.

He placed the sword back at Jack's throat and at last, he spoke aloud. "You, sir are a cream-faced loon." The crowd absolutely erupted in laughter and Jack's ears burned red. He stared at Tom, or the Tom he thought he knew, stunned.

Tom obviously knew the words of *Macbeth* but as prompter, he had read, learned and marvelled at all the wonderful insults that filled many of Will's plays. Now he had a chance to use that knowledge.

"Thou art a fusty nut without a kernel." *Troilus & Cressida*. "A beetle-headed, flap-ear'd knave." That was *Taming of the Shrew*.

"Hey, come now, Tom. No need to be so uncivil."

Tom put his head to one side as if giving his offer serious consideration, before declaring, "I do desire we may be better strangers." *As You Like It*. He racked his brains for any more. "He has not so much brain as ear wax." That was from *Troilus and Cressida* too. Now what about *Henry IV*? Especially where the prince calls Falstaff names. "Thou leathern-jerkin, crystal button, knot-pated, agatering, puke-stocking, caddis-garter, smooth-tongue, Spanish pouch." Tom paused after each individual insult and the crowd started to cheer, just a little ripple of laughter at first but the idea spread like fire, so fairly soon there was a growing crescendo of cheers and laughter after each insult, even louder than the one before. He wasn't even entirely sure what all that meant, especially 'agareting' but it sounded good. Or not good for Jack who had gone a distinct shade of pale.

By now, Tom, the boy, who had been too scared to go on stage just a few short months before, held up his hand and three thousand people fell silent. He held them in the palm of his hand. His actions in combination with Will's words.

A part of Tom, a nicer part, almost began to feel sorry for Jack. But only for a moment. This was the boy who had made his life on the street miserable, who had insulted his mother and his father and who had come here today with the express purpose of destroying the performance. That last point was the most unforgivable. He had been called names all his life and usually he could shrug it off but since coming to The Globe, he could see how much patience, care and love went into the plays. For the gentry in the galleries, this was a bit of light diversion but for the groundlings, the penny that they paid represented at least a day's work, maybe more. Simply by being here, they were losing money and drawing criticism from Puritans who said they should be at work or prayer. It was for them, above all, that Tom felt the need to speak. When idiots like Jack came and tried to shout them down, it was important to stand up and fight back.

From his many hours in the tiring-house working alongside Ned, he knew exactly where the weak points on a garment were and this knowledge together his exhaustive fencing practice, meant he had an unusual advantage over Jack.

With a deft whiplash movement, he slashed at Jack's clothing. The older boy gasped and instinctively patted himself as if looking for money or the site of wounds but Tom's precise strikes had drawn no blood. There was however a clatter as several buttons fell to the floor.

"What the-" began Jack and turned fully to the crowd as slowly his hose sank to his ankles. The crowd roared and screamed with delight, pointing and laughing. Jack, who only now realised what had happened, leaned forward to grab at his clothes in a belated attempt to recover his embarrassment, lost his balance and toppled forward with a cry.

The crowd separated like The Red Sea before Moses and Jack landed face-down in the mud, amongst the all the thrown-away apple-cores and other unwanted items. He slowly stood up, coughing, absolutely plastered head-to-foot in whatever he had fallen in. He grabbed what was left of his clothing and his dignity and spluttering, he stumbled towards the door, the sound of the crowd's laughter ringing in his ears. His embarrassment was clear even under all that mud. By the time he reached the door, he broke into a run.

"Hie thee home, fragment," called Tom to his fast-departing adversary, borrowing one of Edmund's lines from *Romeo and Juliet.*

Jack was not anxious to repeat his humiliation and so resolved not to speak of this to his other nippers. If rumours surfaced about some idiot who had interrupted a play, he would join in with the laughter, albeit nervously. He would not show his face in the playhouse again.

Tom took a couple of deep breaths, returned to his mark on the stage, nodded at Will and the play continued as before. He had managed to stay calm, not lose his temper and most important of all, he had remained in character throughout.

For the final scenes, once Lady Macbeth was dead, Will joined Tom at his usual spot, peeking round the curtain in the tiring-house. "So fair and foul a day I have not seen," noted Will. Rain poured down on the groundlings who stood spellbound, steam rising from their bodies as if their very souls were departing for the next life. They knew Macbeth had committed the worst sin imaginable, they knew he must be punished and of course, since this was a tragedy, they knew the main character would die and yet...and yet. Will had made them care for the man. They had seen him misled, perhaps even cheated by the witches, convinced by his heartless wife and now courageous to the last. They had been standing in the rain for over two hours but no-one left early.

At the end, those in the galleries rose to their feet and clapped. He even spied Pembroke applauding begrudgingly. Tom could have imagined it but their applause seemed to grow louder when he took his bow. The rest of the company were certainly pleased and he received compliments and slaps on the back from Burbage, Armin and even Will.

Backstage later, Tom looked across at Ned's chair, which lay empty and he felt tears well up again.

Heminges put his head round the drape. "Come on, Tom, look lively." He paused, seeing the red circles round Tom's eyes. "He would have wanted you to carry on, you know. Will wants to start planning *Lear*. Says he's got some part for you. A mad beggar or something."

Tom nodded, sniffed. "I'll be out in a minute."

He stood to go but suddenly something caught his eye amongst the rail of garments at the back of the tiring-house. When he wasn't actually in costume for a part, he now donned the finest clothes that someone of his class could afford, reflecting the success of the company. He stepped towards the rail and pushed garments aside as if he was fighting through thick undergrowth. He'd completely forgotten what now met his eyes- the humble tunic that he'd worn that first fateful day when he had been an unwitting stowaway. How shabby it seemed now. There were rips in it and the elbow of the right arm showed sign of heavy-duty darning. His mother could not bear to see him 'walking around in rags' as she put it, so she had mended that hole. He tilted his head slightly to one side as if this helped to see and took a step closer. But she had added something. Either side of the hole and completely unnoticed by Tom until this point, she had put a tiny 'T' and an 'M,' so that she could always identify the garment as his. 'Tom'

He sat back down heavily with the weight of realisation. The old fortune teller had not used witchcraft to divine his name. She'd read it on his tunic.

He wasn't sure if he was relieved or more worried. Alright, she might not have been a witch but her cards had still proved correct. He'd suffered death- not his own, but Ned's. He'd worked with Armin, one of the great Fools of his generation. And he'd played the part of a woman, albeit not a beautiful one. He'd experienced a transformation to a new life in a new world, The Globe and this was due in large part to the words and deeds of its chief magician, Will.

Cuthbert put his head round the drape. "There are some people to see you, Tom."

"Right." Probably delivery orders for *King Lear*. They were already thinking about how to represent the White Cliffs of Dover. That was going to be quite a-

-His thoughts froze as he turned. There were two figures, both of whom were a surprise.

"Mother?"

Will had taken special care to find her a place in the gallery from where she could listen in comfort and safety. She was virtually blind but had been able to follow that day's performance from sound alone had been at first shocked, then disappointed but finally astounded that her boy could do such things. She smiled.

He looked at the other figure standing in front of him- an old man. The eyes that had once been so full of vigour were two faded, milky pools and his face was so heavily-wrinkled now, it was hardly recognisable.

There was a long pause during which neither spoke and then the older man opened his arms and walked forward, enclosing Tom completely. In the depth of this crushing embrace, Tom had to fight for breath and then it came. Through the sweat and other smells, through the thud of his own heartbeat, underneath it all, there it was- the tell-tale scent he remembered from so long ago. It was like a pup recognising its parent.

He hugged back with all his might. The old man before him was no longer able to lift Tom above his shoulders- the boy himself was a young man now but for a split-second in that hug, Tom felt his spirit lift and in his mind he was once again soaring above the crowd.

"But-?" There were so many questions he hardly knew where to start.

Over the following hours, his mother explained how in a recent battle, English forces had overrun a prison in the south-western part of France and had been amazed to find a skeletal figure lurking in the back of a darkened cell. He had not spoken for several weeks but gradually speech had returned and he could tell, in a halting and faint voice how he had not fled as a traitor but had been captured and languished in a French prison as a hostage.

It was like one of Will's comedies with characters who had been separated brought back together but there were darker elements here too and he was suddenly aware of just how little there was left of the man who used to tower over him. The time in prison had stolen his best years. Tom resolved there and then to make the most of however many were left.

Much later, after the exertions of the performance and the celebrations, there was a moment of calm. Tom's parents had made their way home and Tom had promised he would join them soon.

174

Will gathered the main company together, not in the tavern but on the stage of The Globe itself. The warm summer nights had given way to an autumnal chill and the players sat with coats, cloaks and jackets wrapped around their shoulders.

Only Will stood in his habitual black without a coat. It was as if he was still warmed by some kind of inner fire. "Friends, I would like to say a few words. Fear not," he interrupted himself as there were some audible groans from those present. "I am not about to launch into a soliloquy." The groans fell away. "I am 42 years old and no longer a young man." Without thinking, he ran a hand through his hair. Or perhaps where his hair used to be as a sizeable bald patch now adorned his head. "This way of life- it is like a fast-burning candle. Perhaps I could have retained my youth longer if I had followed my father's trade and become a glover or an alderman or a taster of wines."

"You do that readily enough," chipped in Armin, much to the merriment of the company.

Will smiled. "That is true. But I feel my candle, whilst not yet out, is brief." The others fell silent, aware that he was speaking seriously. "In a year or so, The Globe will have competition from Blackfriars Theatre, where Burbage here plans to perform during the winter months. It was a dream of his father's but the neighbours petitioned the Privy Council and it was blocked. This time, Burbage the Younger has somehow managed to charm any dissenting voices.

"They tell me an audience will sit indoors and be prepared to pay sixpence a seat." There were some whistles and some laughter at the ridiculous nature of the enterprise. The only seats for which they could charge sixpence were the tiny number of special so-called 'Lord's gallery seats' or if there was any space in the balcony above the tiring-house if it was not required by musicians. "Yes, I know," he said, acknowledging their reaction. "Perhaps it is foolish; perhaps not. We will see." The noise died.

"The thing is, the life of a playhouse. It's very like a war."

"I beg your pardon?" Tom blurted out without thinking. He could imagine some crowds might be a bit hostile but that seemed an exaggeration.

175

"I mean, the season runs from May to October, weather permitting. Our battles, like the ones in a war, can only be fought in season.

"What I do know is that we are on a moving wheel and must move ourselves or fall. I have a sixth interest invested in the new playhouse and as I perhaps have less energy to write, it is by such measures that I will secure against old age.

"Do not be alarmed," he added, seeking to counteract a few mouths falling open, "I will continue to write as long as I have power to do so but this," he said looking at Tom, "is a young man's game. In five years' time, I will probably be gone."

"Dead?" asked Tom with a quiver of horror.

Will smiled again but this time with only his mouth- the eyes did not join in. "I mean, I will have left London. By then, the fountain," he said, again looking at Tom, "will have become a trickling stream."

Epilogue
(seven years later)

'When sorrows come, they come not single spies
But in battalions.'
(*Hamlet*, Act IV, scene v), l. 74-75).

It was midsummer, right at the end of June. Tom peeked out from the tiring-house and looked up, having to shade his eyes from a sun which beat down on the yard.

He now sported a well-groomed Spanish-style beard, his voice had long since broken and he no longer played female parts. His organisational skills were such that he had been promoted to book-keeper, who kept an eagle-eye over the whole production from the tiring-house.

Here he did not only have to read but write too, and also had to nail a so-called 'platt' to a door on the inner side of the tiring-house, which set out all the necessary details of what props, costumes and special things needed to be remembered for a scene to work.

He was also involved in hiring men for all the lifting and carrying necessary for a production and various jobs like lowering players from the upper trapdoor and firing the cannon. He had to communicate with the stage-keepers, who during performances, peeked round the curtain in front of the tiring-house and kept him informed of what was happening out front and helped sweep up the stage area at the end.

As Will told him, "You have a unique position, Tom. The players only get their sides. No-one holds the whole play. Except me. And now you. The platt is crucial. Whoever holds that, holds all aspects of the play together."

Some of the players had exceedingly poor memories, or so it seemed to Tom, and he was forever reminding players what scene came next or what costume to put on. It was a wonder some of the players did not wander onstage with completely inappropriate costume and start spouting the wrong speech. It did happen but Will was very strict and the system of rehearsals and potential punishments meant such lapses were rare. Players were now a little nervous of Tom- he was not a tyrant but neither was he a boy any longer and could deliver stinging rebukes when necessary. During actual performances, Tom felt the palms of his hands go all clammy just before it began but once the trumpet was blown for the start, it was just like trying to hold on to a runaway horse. The tiring-house became like the worst part of Bedlam, players all wanting to know where they should be and all having questions at the same time, which they expected poor Tom to answer. Instruments, costumes, props, pages of parts left or lost- it became like the centre of a storm.

Tom tried to keep everything as orderly as possible, calmly answering questions, referring to his book if necessary and returning costumes to their correct position on the rails by the back wall.

A few feet away out on the stage, the company were giving a performance of *All Is True* that Will had worked on with fellow poet John Fletcher about King Henry VIII. They had just reached the point where they needed to signal the entrance of the King, played of course by Burbage, at the home of Cardinal Wolsey and for this purpose, a cannon was fired.

These were housed up in the hut and didn't fire a real cannon-ball but one made of paper and cloth. However, for once either the fake ball or the gunpowder and wadding used to fire it did not clear the roof but landed amid the thatch. It may even have been that it was the cover or so-called 'stopple' used to keep the cannon free of dust and moisture that was mistakenly blasted up into the roof.

At first, no-one noticed. The performance continued and the crowd seemed to appreciate the new play. There were always a few pipe smokers amongst the crowd and the effects for pistols and other fireworks often gave off a certain smoky smell.

However, gradually the crowd became aware of the rising smoke and a few voices started to be raised. Burbage was in the middle of one of his big speeches but broke off as the cries of concern escalated and a certain amount of panic broke out.

"FIRE!" The cry grew louder and the groundlings in the yard turned and stumbled towards the main entrance, through which they had come and which now seemed painfully small. There was an instant crush and the people who had been standing pressed ever closer, screaming the names of friends and loved ones to avoid being separated. The nobles up in the galleries had a longer and more difficult route to reach the same door and had to negotiate seats, stairs and more elaborate, bulky clothing that was designed to be looked at, not for speed of movement.

As the smoke built, panic broke out on the stairs as some of the people were petrified that they would not get down in time. By this stage, flames had taken hold on one whole side of the roof and were spreading quickly.

Tom, Will and Gough ran onto the centre of the stage. "We've got to clear the galleries," Will shouted, a hand to his face to prevent the worst of the smoke. "How can we make them MOVE?"

"I have an idea," declared Tom and before they could stop him, he ran back into the smoke-filled tiring-house. He returned moments later with something in his hand.

"What the-" but Gough's question was cut off by the most awful noise imaginable: Tom playing the pipes. He continued with the screeching, raucous cacophony until the nobility fled from their seats, hands pressed over their ears.

In minutes, he stood on the stage gasping for breath, his pipes hanging uselessly at his side. Normally the centre of attention in such a spot, he was now completely ignored.

Suddenly, Will was there again. "Come on, Tom, we must go."

"But-"

"-Now, Tom. There is nothing to be done."

Still he couldn't move, so Will and Cuthbert grabbed his arm and virtually dragged him out. They passed some poor fellow whose breeches caught on fire but luckily, there was plenty of ale still in tankards and bottles, which was used to dampen the flames.

With a final despairing glance over his shoulder, Tom joined the last few to make it out as timbers started to fall and smoke enveloped everything.

There was a half-hearted attempt to form a chain of people to pass buckets of water to try and fight the blaze but the river, although it was in view, was simply too far away and there were no other pumps to hand. The speed of the flames, whipped up by a strong breeze and the dryness of the season made any such attempts futile. With so much of the basic structure made of wood, it was like a huge bonfire, which also claimed a nearby house. In less than an hour, The Globe was gone.

The company, some still a little black around the edges and smelling distinctly smoky, met up at Cross Keys Inn on Grace Church St to the north of the bridge. Years earlier, before The Globe was built, they had even played in the courtyard there. Now that the last 14 years had been wiped out in one fell swoop, as Will might say, they had to consider what to do.

They sat around one of the large, oak tables, tankards of ale set down by a sympathetic landlord, who now had worries of his own, thinking about the money visitors to the playhouse had spent in his establishment over the years.

The company, their faces blackened by ash and smoke, sat in silence and shock. As the flames had leaped higher, huge beams crashed down making the very ground shake like stories of the London quake of 1580 when they say buildings tumbled like toys.

"We were lucky," observed Burbage, his grey hair looking even more so from the smoke.

"Lucky?" Gough couldn't quite believe his ears.

Burbage gave a harsh cough. "There could have been many hundreds killed. Mind you, I heard at least one nobleman say he would risk the flames rather than listen to another second of your pipes, Tom." Tom smiled grimly. "So, what now?" asked Burbage.

Will remained standing, uncowed by fortune. "We rebuild," he declared. "Although we do not have timbers to re-use like last time."

Cuthbert nodded at the memory. "That's true."

"I do have two ideas though," suggested Will.

"What's that?" asked the younger Burbage.

"Tiles rather than thatch." There was some bitter laughter at the economy made in building The Globe that now did not seem such a great idea. "But do not be downhearted," he continued, looking round the group of blackened faces. He was used to motivating this group. He had done it for years and he knew each one of them, better in some ways than his own family. They were his real family. "We are not the poor, struggling players from over a decade ago. We have sufficient funds to rebuild. And we have the talent and the support of many people."

"And what's the second?" asked Burbage senior.

"That you do it without me."

There was another stunned silence.

"But-" began Burbage but Will held up a hand.

"The last 20 years have been like a dream. Now it is time for me to wake. You are like Ariel, Tom." They had been performing *The Tempest* recently in which the magician Prospero keeps a sprite called Ariel to do his bidding on a desert island but finally agrees to let him go at the end. Will gave a gentle smile. "I give you your freedom."

"But I don't want my freedom," stammered Tom hotly, aware of how stupid that sounded and trying to hold back tears and only partly succeeding.

The group fell silent and several of them exchanged anxious glances, not sure if they'd heard Will correctly.

"But..." began Tom, before trailing off.

"But what?" said Will with a tight-lipped smile. "This is a young man's game, you know that. I am a grandfather now and the time has come for me to withdraw. I plan to return home to Stratford, live in New Place and enjoy what years I have left with my family."

"But...what about us?" Tom realised he sounded like a needy child.

"Life will continue. For some time now, I have been working with John Fletcher and he can take my place."

"There will never be another," said Tom with some bitterness.

Will smiled but only with his mouth, not his eyes. "That is not what you thought when you first came here." Tom dropped his gaze in embarrassment as he remembered their chance meeting. He smiled and put his arm around Tom's shaking shoulders. "Tom, my boy." He paused, thinking about his own words. "When Cleopatra looks into her future, she is afraid some boy on stage will shrink her greatness with mere 'squeaks'. You, Tom, are no mere 'squeaking boy.' Now, you are a man, a fine actor, a sound writer, a terrible musician but a wonderful friend. And I shall miss you. But your future lies here. You must instruct a new generation of apprentices. And more than that-"

"-What?"

"Well, all the great parts still await you."

"But…I can't…I'm not…ready."

"It's perfect. Think how well you know the men." He tapped his head. "You've already been inside their minds. Their mind's eye. You can perform them with the understanding gleaned from their female counterparts. Think about it, Tom. You can be Macbeth, knowing what Lady Macbeth is thinking, Romeo, understanding how his love Juliet feels, Hamlet, after experiencing the madness of Ophelia. You are in a truly blessed situation."

Tom sensed his eyes fill with hot tears and did not feel blessed. "But…it won't be the same," he wailed. "Not without you."

"You will always have what matters, Tom. The words. The play's the thing." He raised a tankard and made a toast. "We few, we happy few…we band of…brothers." The last phrase was repeated by the whole company but there was a certain melancholy feel to it too so that as the tankards were raised to lips and silence returned, it felt less like troops massing before a battle as the last time they would be together in this form. A mourning of time passing more than an embracing of times yet to come.

"You write of separated brothers often, do you not?" said Tom. "Or at least brothers that do not treat each other well."

Will fixed him with a stare. "You see much." He nodded. *A Comedy of Errors*, *Hamlet*, *Richard III* even *As You Like It*."

Of his three brothers, he had seen Edmund buried in 1607 only a year after he had spent some time with the company. Then Gilbert last year and now Richard put in the earth but a few months ago.

"Do you remember *Henry VI*, Tom? We were just rehearsing it when you first joined us. I am put in mind of a line or two by the character of Richard, Duke of Gloucester. He plots the demise of his brothers Clarence and Edward:

> I have no brother, I am like no brother;
> And this word "love", which graybeards call divine,
> Be resident in men like one another
> And not in me: I am myself alone.

A sombre silence fell over the group.

"But you are no schemer, Will," said Burbage.

"No but neither have I been a good brother. I did what I could for Edmund but it was not much. Not enough." Will turned to face the group and a faint smile played upon his lips. "I have found my truest sense of brotherhood amongst you, my real family."

In looking for money to pay for the last round of drinks, Tom felt in his pocket and drew out an unexpected object. He held it up to the modest candlelight in the tavern and then placed it on the table. It was a chess-piece. The King, no less.

Will caught sight of this and exchanged a glance with Tom. "Ned would be proud of the player you have become. So, you really will be The King's Men. Mind you, remember not to smoke in James' presence. He's even-"

"-Written a book about it," completed Tom wearily.

"Yes, but how did you-"

"-Just a lucky guess." Everyone was staring at him. "Well, it's just that he has a book on witches, the Divine Right of Kings and how to write poetry, so I just thought why not? Is there anything James hasn't written a book about? Playhouses?"

Will shuddered. "I wouldn't suggest it."

Perhaps there was a way in which Tom could still make his mark. Later, as the company drowned their sorrows and during a lull in conversation, he carefully took the dagger from his belt and glancing round to see no-one was watching, spent a couple of minutes carving something in one of the window panels.

Like Orlando in *As You Like It* carving Rosalind's name on the barks of trees, he wanted to record his feelings for one who had changed his life. Maybe, Will's works would be lost in time but at least his name would endure for a few years at least in one of his favourite places.

Eventually, he stood back to admire his work and nodded in satisfaction. 'William Shaksper'.

Reading List

Books on Shakespeare form an industry all of their own but here are few to get you started. It is a list purposely aimed, for the most part at least, more at students and teachers than academics.

Gary Blackwood, *Shakespeare Stealer* (Dutton, 1998).

Eric Boagey, *Starting Shakespeare* (Collins Educational, 1992).

Peter Brimacombe, *Life in Tudor England* (Pitkin Guides, 2002).

Bill Bryson, *Shakespeare* (Harper Collins, 2009).

Humphrey Carpenter, *Shakespeare Without the Boring Bits* (Viking Penguin, 1994).

Peter Chrisp, *Shakespeare* (Dorling Kindersley, Eyewitness Guides, 2002).

Judith Cook, *Roaring Boys: Shakespeare's Rat Pack* (The History Press, 2006).

Susan Cooper, *King of Shadows* (Bodley Head, 1999).

David Crystal, *The Stories of English* (Penguin/Allen Lane, 2004).

Joy Leslie Gibson, *Squeaking Cleopatras: The Elizabethan Boy Player* (The History Press, 2000).

Alvin B. Kernan, *Shakespeare, the King's Playwright: Theater in the Stuart Court, 1603-1613*

(Yale University Press, 1995).

Frank Kermode, *Shakespeare's Language* (Penguin, 2000).

Lisa Klein, *Lady Macbeth's Daughter* (Bloomsbury USA, 2010).

Jan Mark, *The Stratford Boys* (Hodder Children's Books, 2004).

Charles Nicholls, *The Lodger Shakespeare: His Life on Silver Street* (Penguin, 2009).

Celia Rees, *The Fool's Girl* (Bloomsbury USA, 2010).

James Shapiro, *The Year of Lear: Shakespeare in 1606* (Simon & Schuster, 2015).

Jacqueline Morley and John James, *Shakespearean Theatre* (The Salariya Book Company, 2003).

Potential study/discussion/research topics

- What is the function of each part of a Shakespearean playhouse?

- What does this book tell you about the life of a boy-player?

- Research the historical background of the time and consider what effect this might have had on the plays- The Gunpowder Plot, The Essex Rebellion, James' Act of Union, the outbreaks of plague

- Find out about James' books (on witches, tobacco, The Divine Right of Kings and poetry)

- Everyday life in Shakespearean London, e.g. markets, bear-baiting, public executions.

- Major acting figures of the time, e.g. Richard Burbage, Robert Armin or Will Kempe

- Food/drink in Shakespearean England

- Shakespeare's own life- 'known' facts and myths- Stratford, marriage, children, including conspiracy theories, like what he might have done in the so-called 'wilderness years'

- Shakespeare's plays, poems (e.g. sonnets)- tragedies, comedies, histories and so-called 'problem plays'

- Find out more about the plays *Romeo & Juliet*, *As You Like It*, *Hamlet* and *Macbeth*

- Research one tragic hero, e.g. Macbeth, Hamlet, King Lear, Othello

- Performances in situations other than playhouses, e.g. Royal Palaces, inns/taverns, village greens

http://www.shakespeare-online.com/biography/gunpowderplot.html

Other Works by Scott Pixello

About the Author

I am a Brit living in Germany who loves to read and write. Under a different name, I've had seven books of non-fiction published through three different publishers (one of which is soon to be translated into Chinese- the book not the publishers, that is).

My first book, *Luke, I am Your Father*, a darkly-comic tale of unplanned pregnancy from a male point of view was soon followed by *Memoir of a Gothic Girl*, the chaotic story of a 13-year-old girl who decides to embrace the dark side of life and 'go Goth' as a way of coping with pressures at home and school. *Live Long and Prospero* (about a bunch of lunatics on a lighthouse in 1983) features a Captain with a *Star Trek* obsession and *Gagfest UK* is a darker tale of a stand-up comedian who has the deal with the ultimate heckler. *Rainbow* is about a very special farmyard animal that can accurately predict football scores. These books are not part of a series.

There are no pictures of me on the Net and I do not Tweet, have my own website or even own a mobile phone (gasp). I could tell you my real name but then I'd have to kill you and no-one wants that. However, I'm not a complete recluse. I am on Goodreads and Facebook and if you 'friend' me on FB, then you will hear about new releases/other vital news before anyone else.

Remember as the Dalai Lama once said, "there are only two things you must do in life:

Live…AND BUY MY BOOKS." And when he says 'my books' he really means 'my' books coz I don't think he's written any himself.

Oops, just Googled the Old DL & it turns out he has. Basically, buy mine first and if you've any money left over, you could try his stuff. Coz it's probably quite good. Although my books are funnier.

For more on Scott Pixello see…
www.facebook.com/scott.pixello
http://www.goodreads.com/author/show/7114466.Scott_Pixello

14220549R00111

Printed in Poland
by Amazon Fulfillment
Poland Sp. z o.o., Wrocław